WADSWORTH PHILOSOPHERS SERIES

ON

THOREAU

Stephen Hahn
William Paterson University

Wadsworth
Thomson Learning

Australia • Canada • Mexico • Singapore • Spain
United Kingdom • United States

Printed in the United States of America
1 2 3 4 5 6 7 03 02 01 00 99

For permission to use material from this text, contact us:
Web: http://www.thomsonrights.com
Fax: 1-800-730-2215
Phone: 1-800-730-2214

For more information, contact:
Wadsworth/Thomson Learning
10 Davis Drive
Belmont, CA 94002-3098
USA
http://www.wadsworth.com

ISBN: 0-534-57613-3

Contents

Preface

While writing this book between January and August of 1999, I lived in a small house among the Hopatcong Hills in the "ribbed north end of/ Jersey/ with its isolate lakes and/ valleys" celebrated by William Carlos Williams (*Collected Poems*, Vol. I: 217). This autobiographical note is significant because, having completed the book, I realize that it takes an added coloration from this placement, not unlike Thoreau's own, on the margins of American life. For though I commuted most days some forty miles to a job in university administration within sight of the skyline of Manhattan, I also lived, many days and most nights, close to the sort of solitude one imagines Thoreau sought at Walden. During the same months, I have also frequently had gentle companionship, tucked in these hills, with two people who have helped me to orient myself in a way Thoreau speaks of doing. I have tried to think with Thoreau about some of the central issues of human life from this vantage, while extracting from his writing what I believe are representative themes, and to engage the reader in a similar process of thinking. Throughout, one will find Thoreau insisting on the general necessity of a radical reorientation of thought and action which is individual to each person who undertakes it. The requirement is universal, the enactment personal. As a result, Thoreau is less inclined to tell you what to think that to raise the question of when to think and why. I hope my treatment of his writing here will alter, if only slightly, the reader's estimation of the importance of this question. I hope too that it will alter for some readers the notion that Thoreau was only solitary by revealing the power of his empathic imagination and his concern for community, which is at least as important as his concern for the preservation of wildness, as one enlivens the other.

Several people heard or read portions of this book as it developed and offered insightful comments or encouragement, for which I am grateful. Among them are Catarina Edinger, Daniel Kolak, Robert J. Kloss, and Albert McDowell. Chrystena Chrzanowski, one of the two companions mentioned above, read the whole manuscript several times over, raised questions about meaning and style, proofread successive versions, and gave thoughtful and tactful support throughout the process of composition. Carmen Pardo and Judy Norton helped to resolve problems with formatting. Any errors and infelicities that remain are solely my own.

This book is dedicated to my two companions, Chrystena and Margaret Mei, who have taught me much about losing and finding.

Hopatcong, New Jersey
August 30, 1999

1
Thoreau's Life and Thought

Thoreau as Philosopher and Thinker

"With thinking we may be beside ourselves in a sane sense"—
(*Walden* 91)

Henry David Thoreau is one of the more popularly known
nineteenth-century American writers, eclipsed perhaps only by Edgar
Allan Poe. Both are remembered for being at odds with the
mainstream of their culture. Yet while Poe is most consistently
remembered as the poet of urban alienation ("The Man of the Crowd")
and claustrophobic imaginings ("Murders in the Rue Morgue" and
"The Cask of Amontillado"), Thoreau is recalled as a free spirit of the
woods. His phrases about the person who "hears a different drummer"
(*Walden* 217) and about the preservation of wilderness are
commonplaces quoted in many a graduation speech and poster.
However familiar these words have become, they are but touchstones
among the nearly two million words Thoreau actually wrote.
Likewise, the more well-remembered episodes of his life—his
"sojourn" of two years, two months, and two days at Walden Pond,
his night in jail for refusing to pay taxes, or his flogging of
schoolchildren as a teacher at the Center School in Concord—may
lead us to simplify his complex character and to consider him only an
eccentric who, in a great American tradition, can be tolerated exactly
to the degree that he and his thoughts, however "measured," do

1

remain "far away" ("Resistance to Civil Government" 217).

In his own time, Thoreau was so regarded by some. One early critic called him a "Yankee Diogenes" after the great cynic of ancient Greece (Briggs 314), and his close associate and mentor Ralph Waldo Emerson expressed his disappointment that Thoreau did not turn his energy to greater practical pursuits and attempt to achieve greater intellectual influence during his lifetime ("Thoreau" 331-32). In our time, however, the idea of Thoreau as a philosopher survives. The philosopher Stanley Cavell considers Thoreau, for instance, in *The Senses of Walden*, in comparison to the Viennese philosopher Ludwig Wittgenstein. And Thoreau has had an influence in the development of social philosophy upon figures such as Mohandas Ghandi and Martin Luther King, Jr. These various points of comparison and influence begin to suggest a more complex figure than public memory brings to the fore when his words are quoted.

In his complexity, Thoreau embodies and exposes contradictions that can be said to inform life in the United States. On one hand, he seems to represent a figure who turns his back on public life to experiment with "life in the woods." On the other, he seems to represent a revolutionary impulse to overturn the social order—for he spoke fervently in favor of John Brown, who had violently attacked the U.S. Arsenal at Harpers Ferry, Virginia, in 1859, and on the occasion of Brown's execution in December of that year. Moreover, he did not confine himself to words—as he accused others of doing— but committed himself to actions, such as assisting fugitive slaves and one member of John Brown's cohort in escaping to Canada. If Thoreau seems like a pacifist because of his opposition to war, such as that of the U.S. against Mexico in 1846-48, he seems at the same time militant in his opposition. And so he embodies a contradiction of thought for which it would be difficult to find a close example among his predecessors. At least in this respect, he may be considered a "paradigmatic individual," to borrow the phrase the philosopher Karl Jaspers used to describe four philosophers who were Thoreau's own great, if remote, teachers: Socrates, Buddha, Confucius, and Jesus. What Jaspers calls the "historicity and uniqueness" of these teachers is a quality that Thoreau, in an admittedly smaller way, shares (*The Great Philosophers*, Vol. 1, 3).

Like them, Thoreau expresses his thoughts largely in the form of narratives—parables and fables—from which precepts can be drawn. And so, like them, he is less apparently systematic than we have come to expect philosophers to be. He was less concerned, as well, with

2

deciding the great philosophical issues or developing a separate and more consistent logic than what was offered by language and action in the observed world around him. At times, indeed, it seems that these issues come to his mind in the midst of his telling a story only to be let go or to lead to other musings. (For instance, he asks in the middle of one such story, "What sort of space is it which separates a man from his fellows and makes him solitary?" [*Walden* 90], only to conclude by telling how he met one man on the way to the market who asked him how he could afford to "give up so many comforts of life" and yet went home to bed while the other traveled all night on his errands.) As a contemporary critic says, writing of Thoreau, whatever one may make of him in terms of formal or academic philosophy, his writing "delineate[s] a series of stances toward the world that are, in the broadest sense, philosophical" (Bickman 100). Thoreau himself is more emphatic: "To be a philosopher is not merely to have subtle thoughts, nor even to found a school, but so to love wisdom as to live according to its dictates, a life of simplicity, independence, magnanimity, and trust" (*Walden* 9).

It is beyond the scope of this series to make a full inquiry into how, historically, two different models of being a philosopher diverged. But surely they did: Philosophy tends to be regarded as concerned either with things prior to action or even to thought (determining the possible forms of thought, for instance) or with those subsequent to action (evaluating what is given, but not choosing to alter it). Philosophers have come to be regarded as standing apart from the action—and Thoreau will have something to say and exemplify in that respect—so that changes in the model are somewhat remarkable. Examples of those who diverge from the standard model could be cited: Sartre, perhaps, or Camus; Russell or Chomsky. Each of them is engaged in action as well as thought. But interestingly, what some do as philosophers is remote from what they do as public persons. In any case, Thoreau seems both a little out of step and a little out of the sequence of time, more like the paradigmatic individual than like the formal philosopher—not the least because his writing so often exemplifies the dictum that knowledge ends in wonder.

Thoreau may not be unique in contrasting the formal pursuits of philosophy with qualities of life such as the four mentioned in the quotation above. Yet his pursuit of living according to this definition and his having written so compellingly of that pursuit have ensured his significance for several generations of readers. Each of these generations has returned to his writing with renewed interest that is not merely, sometimes not even, academic. And each has found one or more faces of Thoreau of particular interest and use. This volume attempts to give insight into several facets of his life and writing, beginning with a short biographical sketch.

College Education and Early Life

David Henry Thoreau, as he was first named, graduated nineteenth in a class of 43 from Harvard College at the age of 20, in August of 1837. (Commencements were then traditionally held in late summer.) On entering Harvard he had barely passed the entrance examination. Graduating almost in the dead middle of his class, he obviously had not distinguished himself to a great degree by the standards of the college in the interval. Nevertheless, Thoreau did participate in the intellectual portion of the commencement by joining a debate or "conference" on "The Commercial Spirit of the Times." There he presented an essay that commended the beauty over the utility of nature, presaging a theme of his later writing. It is tempting to think, for the sake of composing a neatly prophetic narrative, that Thoreau drew inspiration from Ralph Waldo Emerson's famous Phi Beta Kappa Address, delivered on August 31. Biographers believe, however, that Thoreau had already returned from Cambridge to his hometown of Concord, some twelve miles to the West, following his role in the commencement, perhaps forecasting other aspects of his later development. (See Richardson, *A Life* 8-23.) Of the relationship between Thoreau and Emerson, more in a moment, but first: What did going to Harvard mean, and how did Thoreau get there?

Henry was the only one of four children (including a brother, John, and two sisters, Helen and Sophia) to attend college, although members of his family seem to have been quite literate and involved in the affairs of their community. (Sophia assisted in editing his work after his death; all three taught school, which then required no degree.) Henry had been born in Concord and had lived in Boston, where his father taught school, and Chelmsford, Massachusetts, where his father ran a store, before the family returned to Concord in 1823, when he was still a child—a return he recalls in *Walden*. There his father took over a pencil-making business founded by his wife Cynthia's brother, Charles Dunbar. Cynthia took in boarders to supplement the family's income, but she also engaged in charity work in the town. Henry attended a private "infant" school and the public Center School of Concord where he would later teach briefly. Subsequently, John and

Henry attended a private academy in Concord, and Henry attended lectures at the Concord Lyceum—an institution dedicated to the education or "improvement" of the community at large, common to nineteenth-century towns of New England. Neither Henry's nor John's education was indifferent to this point, but it was Henry who was preferred to continue, while his brother and two sisters went to work teaching school. In contemporary terms, which can only be approximate, his background was more or less middle-class. It took some time for the family to establish and own a permanent home and develop a family business, but they worked in the as-yet-unprofessionalized professions of the middle class. Eventually, the family owned a significant home on Main Street in Concord, which Thoreau helped to build and where he lived, supporting his mother and sister after his father's death in 1859 until his own early death in 1862.

Admission to Harvard was in no way as competitive in 1833 as it is today, although the ratio of college students to the general population was phenomenally smaller (about 1:1300 compared to 1:20). A college education was simply not a requirement for positions in business and industry, teaching, or for that matter anything else except the established ministry and medicine. The pay of the faculty at Harvard, and other colleges, the physical plant, technology, and other things that increase the cost of attending college simply did not make it so comparatively expensive as to exclude all but the privileged. Harvard College had been in existence for almost two hundred years, but such as thing as "teaching" (however one might define that) barely existed. The method of undergraduate education was recitation. Educational practice reflected the etymology of the word "college": "reading together." Students amassed points for the completion of assignments (and lost them for misbehavior, including cutting chapel) that eventually totaled more than ten thousand on graduation. The supposedly formative "curriculum" of the modern college or university, division of the faculty into a multitude of disciplines, and consequent distribution requirements, did not yet exist. Thoreau's studies were mainly in languages (Greek, Latin, French, German, and Spanish), the history of English literature, mathematics, and philosophy. Besides providing him with the opportunity to study languages in depth, perhaps the most influential aspect of undergraduate practice (as for many undergraduates) was the exercise of regularly writing short themes and compositions.

In 1835-36, Thoreau took leave from college for a term to teach

5

school (for the first time, apparently to earn money to support himself) in nearby Canton, Massachusetts, where he lived with the Unitarian minister (later to become Catholic convert) <u>Orestes Brownson</u> for six weeks, studying German with him. The following spring he took a briefer leave due to illness, which biographers believe may have signaled the onset of the tuberculosis from which he would ultimately die. In July of 1836, he was a member of the choir at the dedication of the Concord Bridge Memorial (to the soldiers of the Revolutionary War which—at least in patriotic mythography—began there at the Battle of Lexington and Concord), singing Emerson's "Concord Hymn" to the traditional tune of "Old Hundred." For six weeks that summer, he lived with his college friend Charles Stearns Wheeler in a hut on the shore of Flint's Pond in Lincoln, Massachusetts, and later he visited New York City with his father to sell pencils. The next year saw his graduation. For all else we might know from the common images of his later life—burning the town woods by accident, spending a night in jail, living alone at Walden, and dying an early death of tuberculosis—that life might seem haphazard. Surely it had its troubles. Did it have coherence?

Finding a Vocation and Living a Life

Like most college graduates, Thoreau had to elect some paths to follow on entering adult life. It is important to recognize how some of these opened or did not open for him, how he chose among those available, if only to counter some myths—such as that he was impractical to the degree that his writing was really a compensation for his failure to find a vocation, constitutionally incapable of close, personal relationships, or Concord-bound for want of interest in environments beyond his hometown.

Following his graduation, Henry obtained a very well paying job teaching at the Center School in Concord. The position paid over $500 a year, more than enough to establish a middle-class life. He immediately broadened his associations among a group of prominent "Transcendentalists," a loosely affiliated group of thinkers including Emerson and Margaret Fuller (with whom he would have long personal relationships), and he began keeping a journal that would amount to some two million words in the next 25 years. He also made the first of his innovations in his family's pencil-making business, putting his library privileges at Harvard to good use in discovering a method to harden pencil-lead (graphite), and innovating a method of grinding graphite more finely. Within a few weeks, he resigned his position as teacher, after "flogging" students on orders from an overseer of the school, but he (soon joined by his brother John) continued to pursue teaching positions.

Each of these three areas of endeavor—teaching, writing, and pencil-making—represented lively possibilities for a career. Two of them, teaching and writing, of course, comported well with each other. Within a year, John and Henry planned to go to Kentucky to teach school together, but abandoned plans when John obtained a position in Roxbury (then an outlying farming community near Boston, later a middle-class suburb, and today a sprawling, impoverished ghetto). Henry looked for a teaching position in Maine, opened a small private school at home, and finally (with assistance from Emerson) took over Concord Academy, from which he had graduated. By the spring of 1838, he was secretary and curator of the Concord Lyceum (arranging lectures there), where he gave his own lecture in April, on the topic of "Society." Again, within a year, the enrollment at the Academy grew (as it would only do if the instruction and conduct of the school were well regarded), and John joined him in teaching there. Together, the brothers made an excursion to the headwaters of the Merrimack River (one of the more significant rivers in the industrial development of the northeast) in the White Mountains of New Hampshire, by way of its tributary Concord River—a journey and "friendship" he memorialized in *A Week on the Concord and Merrimack Rivers* (1849), written principally during his stay at Walden.

Thoreau continued to thrive in the literary environment and in teaching school until John's ill health contributed to the closing of the Academy in April 1841. In the meantime, he and John had unfortunately fallen in love with the same woman, 17-year-old Ellen Sewell of Scituate, Massachusetts, who rejected proposals from John and Henry in turn in 1840. For both to fall in love with the same woman and both to be rejected must have been both unhappy and fortunate, since neither would have to live with the other's actually marrying the woman he loved. If the rejection closed one path to Henry, that of the prospect of marriage, if not necessarily on a permanent basis, it did not preclude continuing "literary" friendships, including the one with Emerson. After closing the Academy, Henry worked for Emerson as housekeeper while seeking a more permanent situation (he contemplated purchasing a farm) for two years (1841-1843), and then spent half a year on Staten Island, New York, tutoring Emerson's brother William's children and seeking literary connections in New York City. Along the way, he met Nathaniel and Sophia Hawthorne, Horace Greeley, Henry James, Sr., and other important figures. He also tragically lost his brother in January 1842 to "lockjaw" (rapidly progressive muscular paralysis) resulting from an infected razor cut, and that loss was among the most deeply felt of his life.

Moving to Walden Pond in 1845 represented an indirect benefit of his long relationship with Emerson. For some time, at least since the days of living with Charles Stearns Wheeler at Flint's Pond (1836), Thoreau had intermittently sought some such arrangement. Emerson owned land on the shore of Walden and Emerson's permission enabled him to build a small, one room cabin there; and there he composed the first drafts of *A Week,* began *Walden,* and confirmed his vocation as a writer. He would not—few writers do—make a living exclusively from writing, but from occasional work such as surveying and for a time again tending to the affairs of the Emerson household (while Emerson traveled in Europe). His local notoriety continued to accrue from his episode with the jailer, his growing of prize pumpkins, and his provocative lectures—including "Civil Disobedience" or "Resistance to Civil Government" (1848). He traveled widely, contrary to a mythography that views him as place-bound. Trips to Cape Cod and the Allagash wilderness of Maine resulted eventually in published writing and posthumously in two volumes edited by his sister (arrangements for which were made in 1861, when he knew he was dying). Otherwise, he traveled to Perth Amboy, New Jersey (on a surveying commission), New York City (visiting his friend Bronson Alcott and meeting the poet Walt Whitman), the White Mountains and Maine, and finally to Minnesota (with Horace Mann, Jr.) pursuing health and his long interest in the situation of Native Americans. Having long been active in anti-slavery activities, including those of the so-called "underground railroad," he met the radical abolitionist and revolutionary John Brown in Concord in 1857. After Brown's attack on Harpers Ferry in 1859, he championed Brown as a martyr to the cause of the abolition of slavery. Throughout these years, he not only maintained and developed his literary connections but he developed scientific ones as well, corresponding with and contributing specimens to Louis Agassiz, perhaps the foremost natural historian in the United States at the time. Throughout his life he collected Indian artifacts and explored Indian languages, and (some would argue) discovered a second, belated vocation as a more methodical naturalist. By the time he wrote

8

the last words in his journal in November 1861, there were some two million of them, including several books in manuscript. He lived until May 6, 1862, when he died after succumbing to the progressive advance of tuberculosis and was buried May 9 in Concord.

Throughout his life of forty-four years, Thoreau showed remarkable adaptability to practical affairs when he needed to turn to them to support himself or his family. He surveyed much of the land in Concord, made innovations in the manufacturing methods of the family business and helped to build two family homes, and he tended for two rather long periods to the practical affairs of the Emerson household. He had a wide range of friends; was devoted to the cause of justice and remained involved in the affairs of his community. He traveled, lectured, and observed the natural landscape throughout New England and beyond. He urged people to simplify the contrivances of their lives, to act from principle, to examine their condition, to do justice. "Simplicity, independence, magnanimity, and trust" were the words he chose to characterize the philosopher (*Walden* 9). His own simplicity and complexity are indicated as well by two sentences, spaced a few sentences apart in the text of *Walden*, as by any others:

We belong to the community.

No doubt another *may* also think for me; but it is not therefore desirable that he should do so to the exclusion of my thinking for myself. (31)

For Thoreau, "the community" is as near as the nearest person assisting us in building a house and as distant as the traces of former inhabitants and the texts of ancient philosophers. But the conditions of community never permit us not to be responsible for and responsive to ourselves, or what is the community composed of? If it is characteristic of paradigmatic individuals that they find the revelatory and revolutionary potential within the premises of their own known communities and challenge members of their communities to authentic reflection—meaning a practice and habit of thinking, "beside ourselves" if need be. Like such individuals, Thoreau knew and attempted to transform the traditions of his own culture, especially as it derived from the New Testament record of the teaching of Jesus and as it was embedded in the speech of his country-men and women. Among other things, Thoreau seems to have created the paradigm of the individual who is both "militant" and "pacifist"—and therefore to have created a path or practice followed in some part by Ghandi and King. He also exemplifies a set of stances toward life in a democratic society, open to the future and somewhat troubled by its past. This includes not only the past represented by specific religious content, for instance, but also, as Stanley Cavell argues, that represented by the "mysteriousness of ownership" as a kind of religious fetish enduring into the present (see "Captivity and Despair" 401). As chief surveyor of much of the property in Concord for some time, he was immersed in the process of the definition and transmission of property. Yet he maintained himself at arm's length from ownership. "Beside himself" as he must necessarily have been (and we will see further the resonance of that phrase) he was so, for the most part, coherently.

Relationship to Emerson

If Thoreau did not stay to hear Emerson's Phi Beta Kappa address that August day at the Harvard commencement exercises in 1837, the two were already known to each other. Soon they would develop a relationship that would be hard to characterize either as that of mutual friends or as that of mentor and apprentice. Emerson now stands so pre-eminent in the canon of American literary history (and, to some extent, American philosophy) that, like his famous imaginary "transparent eye-ball" in *Nature* (*Essays and Lectures* 10), nearly everything can be said to flow in and out of him for a century or more after his death. Estimates of his influence may be infected with hyperbole, but not much. Thoreau's career as a writer of journals, if not as a writer altogether, is frequently traced to Emerson's question to him about whether he kept a journal. Indeed, the journal begins by memorializing, anonymously to be sure, that query. And it was Emerson who gave the most influential canonical judgment regarding Thoreau in his eulogy:

> Had his genius been only contemplative, he had been fitted to his life, but with his energy and practical ability he seemed born for great enterprise and for command: and I so much regret the loss of his rare powers of action, that I cannot help counting it a fault in him that he had no ambition. Wanting this, instead of engineering for all America, he was the captain of a huckleberry party. Pounding beans is good to the end of pounding empires one of these days, but if at the end of years, it is still only beans!— ("Thoreau" 331-32)

10

Such a judgment in an America that was (and is) about the business of pounding empires amounts nearly to condemnation rather than a statement of heart-felt personal disappointment. And readers forget that Emerson lifts his tone at the end of the eulogy to compare Thoreau to the flower "*Edelweisse*, which signifies, *Noble Purity*" (333). Still it is indicative of the difference between Emerson and Thoreau to focus just on this point of the topic of "empires," for Thoreau had written in *Walden*:

> But the only true America is that country where you are at liberty to pursue such a mode of life as may enable you to do without these [tea, coffee, meat], and where the state does not compel you to sustain the slavery and war and other superfluous expenses which directly or indirectly result from the use of such things. (*Walden* 138)

Here in his disparagement of the commodities of empire, as in many other places, Thoreau is as radically resistant to the idea and practice of "empire" (real or imaginary) as any critic of America before or since. To a contemporary reader, and to Thoreau's contemporaries, it may seem that to think of tea and coffee and meat as the products of injustice is to treat an accidental relationship as an essential one. Could not these products of empire be had without slavery or war? Perhaps. Are they so had? Not likely. The plantation system, the system of ownership of means to these ends, may change in some aspects without changing essentially. For Thoreau, a merely superficial change is no change in the deeper relationship, and he was far more attuned to the personal implications of political relationships between people—either close up or across distances of oceans or North and South, East and West—than was Emerson.

There was, of course, confluence between the ideas of the two, which can be illustrated by citing the text of "The American Scholar" as well as any of Emerson's essays. First and foremost, and among the most celebrated of Emerson's assertions, is the emphasis on "experience" rather than mere book-learning in the life of the scholar. "Only so much do I know, as I have lived," Emerson writes, "so much only do I know of life as I know by experience..." (*Essays and Lectures* 60). Here is a theme he shares with Thoreau. Then he continues the last sentence: "...so much of wilderness have I vanquished and planted, or so far have I extended my being, my

11

dominion" (60). Emerson offers a spiritualized version of the political doctrine and geo-political trend that came to be known as "Manifest Destiny." One may claim that in fact it is spiritualized, metaphorical, and therefore not equivalent to an endorsement of crude plantocracy, capitalism, and empire building. But why choose just these metaphors to represent a world of spirit, and what difference does it make that Thoreau and Emerson seem to diverge in their choices of language with respect to this theme? For Thoreau is always concerned to avoid the illusion that the mere self can impose an order, "dominion," or "empire" over either fellow human beings or the natural world:

> I desire that there may be as many different persons in the world as possible; but I would each one be very careful to find out and pursue his own way, and not his father's or his mother's or his neighbor's instead. (*Walden* 48)

> We need the tonic of wildness....At the same time that we are earnest to explore and learn all things, we require that all things be mysterious and unexplorable, that land and sea be infinitely wild, unsurveyed and unfathomed by us because unfathomable....We need to witness our own limits transgressed, and some life pasturing freely where we never wander. (*Walden* 212)

> The West of which I speak is but another name for the Wild; and what I have been preparing to say is, that in Wildness is the preservation of the World....It was because the children of the Empire were not suckled by the wolf that they were conquered and displaced by the children of the northern forest who were. ("Walking" 112-13)

> I would not have every man nor every part of a man cultivated, any more than I would have every acre of the earth cultivated: part will be tillage, but the greater part will be meadow and forest, not only serving an immediate use, but preparing a mould against a distant future, by the annual decay of the vegetation which it supports. ("Walking" 126)

Partly we encounter Thoreau wearing the hat of the naturalist here and drawing tropes from "pounding beans." If nothing else, the comparison to Emerson should raise for us the question of how we are to regard a philosophy that seems to be founded in an ecological perspective, and to try to understand what that perspective may entail. It also raises questions about how we value what contemporary discourse calls difference and diversity. And those questions might be formulated to ask what impels, on the one hand, the desire for dominion, intellectual or political, residing in Emerson's form of expression as compared to what might be called the desire for relation residing in Thoreau's. Are they compatible with each other, and is either sustainable by itself?

Both the confluence and the divergence of Emerson's and Thoreau's perspectives can be gauged at a further depth by citing a long passage that articulates the central theme of "The American Scholar," the theme of the "One Man." Emerson writes:

> The old fable covers a doctrine new and ever sublime; that there is One Man;—present to all particular men partially, or through one faculty; and that you must take the whole society to find the whole man. Man is not a farmer, or a professor, or an engineer, but he is all. Man is priest, and scholar, and statesman, and producer, and soldier. In the *divided* or social state, these functions are parcelled [sic] out to individuals, each of whom aims to do his stint of joint work, whilst each other performs his. The fable implies, that the individual, to possess himself, must return from his own labor to embrace all the other laborers. But unfortunately, this original unit, has been so distributed to multitudes, has been so minutely divided and peddled out, that it is spilled into drops, and cannot be gathered. The state of society is one in which the members have suffered amputation from the trunk, and strut about so many walking monsters,—a good finger, a neck, a stomach, an elbow, but never a man. (*Essays and Lectures* 54)

The fable of the division of the "One Man" represents a version of the story of the Fall of Man without the intervening action of original sin. It has parallels in diverse other texts, such as Milton's adaptation of the story of Osiris in "Areopagitica" (*Selected Prose* 234-36), the imagery of the body politic in Shakespeare's *Coriolanus* (e.g., 1.1. 100-67), and Marx's discussion of the division of labor (*Capital* XIV: 276-303, especially 289). The theme of the diminishment of human possibility as people become reduced to discrete functions, symbolized here by body parts, and lack integration is a theme common to both Thoreau and Emerson. We might observe, however, that each approaches the theme from a different perspective. For Emerson, the divided state is a given, commensurate with the "state of society," and it affects even the status of "Man Thinking":

> In this distribution of functions, the scholar is the delegated intellect. In the right state, he is, *Man Thinking*. In the degenerate state, when the victim of society, he tends to become a mere thinker, or, still worse, the parrot of other men's thinking. (54)

The distinction is between a person ("mere thinker") whose function is simply to think abstractedly, without connection to another function and one who integrates all the functions of "Man" and so thinks, to borrow parallel phrases from Wordsworth, "not as a lawyer, a mariner, an astonomer, or a natural philosopher, but as a Man" ("Preface." *Lyrical Ballads* [1802] 257-258). Emerson's approach to the theme is to begin with the assumption that the state of society requires the division. The division must then be overcome, not by altering actual social relations, but by incorporating into thinking a broader view of all nature, so that "the ancient precept 'Know Thyself,' and the modern precept, 'Study Nature,' become at last one maxim" (56).

Whether Emerson makes an adequate transition from his statement of the problem to his solution is a question that can remain, for us, unanswered. He begins with the assumption, however, that what can be stated in the abstract can be resolved in the abstract. His mode of exposition is something like "thinking aloud" in which those who hear or overhear his thinking are implicitly invited to think along with him, which is to think indirectly. Thoreau differs from Emerson, I would argue, by beginning in something more like an active social relation, referred to by Wordsworth, of "a man speaking to men"— colloquial, digressive, argumentative, and dialectical or dialogical where Emerson is magisterial and monological. He differs, also, by beginning not with the abstract statement of the general case but with particular observations:

> I see young men, my townsmen, whose misfortune it is to have inherited farms, houses, barns, cattle, and farming tools; for these are more easily acquired than got rid of. Better if they had been born in the open pasture and suckled by a wolf, that they might

see with clearer eyes what field they were called to labor in. Who made them serfs of the soil? (*Walden* 2)

Emerson would say that Thoreau here points to the condition of those who have sunk "into the farmer, instead of Man on the farm," but his view is metaphysical (without agency the farmer "sees his bushel and cart and sinks..."). In contrast, Thoreau's is existential and political, implying that someone (or the conditions existing among some people) causes these relations to exist. The consequence is, I believe, that Thoreau's approach enables us to conceive that social, and hence epistemological, relations can be altered while Emerson's approach tends to refer us back to the epistemological and behind that to the metaphysical only. It is not too much to say, I think, that Emerson quickly generalizes from existing conditions to abstractions such as "fate" and "character," thereby making the existential appear as the essential. Without what may be Thoreau's running and subversive commentary on his text (and there is some evidence that Thoreau specifically alludes to and undercuts Emerson in a number of passages), Emerson's thought might seem more stable in its premises than it is.

Thoreau does not, however, typically argue directly against Emerson. Considering the relationship of subordination between them, in which Emerson the proper landholder employed Thoreau for two substantial periods of time and allowed him the use of his land on the shores of Walden, there may be in Thoreau's attitude toward him both personally and intellectually a sense that one does not bite the hand that feeds—or not too obviously. One can imagine also that Emerson's discourse gained priority in their environment without being reductively psychoanalytic: Emerson was first on the scene as a writer. Emerson's words dominated in the Lyceum that Thoreau ran for a time and in the journal for which Thoreau was something like what we would today call the "managing editor." If Emerson's ownership of land at Walden enabled Thoreau to build a cabin and live there, Thoreau's time and labor (in 1847-48, for instance, when he took care of the Emerson household) enabled Emerson to travel to Europe. Their relationship suggests a kind of symbiosis but lacks full reciprocity. As we have seen, Thoreau begins his journal noting the prompting of a friend to do so, but the friend (most probably Emerson) remains anonymous. Thus even in this relatively private medium Thoreau is oblique in his admission of personal influence.

Finally, with few exceptions (perhaps those of his brother John

15

and his later hero John Brown), Thoreau is oblique about specifically personal relationships in his writing. When he echoes most closely Emerson's words, and alters or extenuates their meaning by a change of context, he is following something like a characteristic pattern of discourse that goes "people say/think X, but the truth is Y." Such discourse is oriented toward a prior discourse as a point of departure, but the figure is one of departure, striking out into a territory of new meaning against old. So Thoreau in his relationship to Emerson seems silently to acknowledge him as a precursor while at the same time claiming that his current thought is not sponsored by any prior commitment of intellectual allegiance to some else's thought.

Unsponsored Thought

"Genius is not a retainer to any emperor"—(*Walden* 39)

In the world of intellectual work, much thinking and writing is "sponsored" by institutions, agencies, or constituencies that have an interest in the formation and outcome of the process. When the ideal is a disinterested pursuit of knowledge or truth, as it ostensibly is in the academic world, fairly elaborate pains are taken to specify how what is called "academic freedom" is maintained and whose interests may be served by thought and discourse. The ideal is that even knowledge or truth contrary to a vested interest shall be pursued or discovered. Writers and thinkers, like other kinds of workers, frequently need to make a living, which involves an adjustment of means to ends, as in the instance of tailoring one's thought and writing to serve the ends of a market or client. So writers and thinkers who wish to maintain their independence are frequently jealous to guard against the influence of "the hand that feeds" them.

Thoreau's own concern to maintain an independence of mind that would enable him to "speak somewhere *without* bounds" (*Walden* 216) is reflected in many places, but pointedly here in a parable about a basket maker:

> Not long since, a strolling Indian went to sell baskets at the house of a well-known lawyer in my neighborhood. "Do you wish to buy any baskets?" he said. "No, we do not want any," was the reply. "What!" exclaimed the Indian as he went out the gate, "do you mean to starve us?" Having seen his industrious white neighbors so well off,—that the lawyer had only to weave

16

arguments, and by some magic wealth and standing followed, he had said to himself; I will go into business; I will weave baskets; it is a thing which I can do. Thinking that when he had made baskets he would have done his part, and then it would be the white man's to buy them. He had not discovered that it was necessary for him to make worth the other's while to buy them, or at least make him think that it was so, or to make something else which it would be worth his while to buy. I too had woven a kind of basket of delicate texture [traditionally, Thoreau is taken here as referring to his first book, *A Week*], but I had not made it worth any one's while to buy them. Yet not the less, in my case, did I think it worth my while to weave them, and instead of studying how to make it worth men's while to buy my baskets, I studied rather how to avoid the necessity of selling them. (*Walden* 12)

The stereotype of the "strolling Indian" may be partially excused by the fact that Thoreau makes himself (at least initially) the butt of the joke. As elsewhere in the "Economy" chapter of *Walden*, the point has to do with the adjustment of means to ends and what steps are necessary to pursue the form of liberty Thoreau identifies with "true America." It would be easy, and erroneous, to identify this avoidance as an avoidance of work—for he avowedly wishes to keep making "baskets." Rather, the object is to avoid (one should say here, not absolutely but as much as possible) participating in what we have come to call the "cycle of exchange" or "commodity culture"—what Wordsworth in one of his great sonnets had called simply "getting and spending" ("The World is Too Much with Us")—in order to retain the freedom to make "baskets" according to one's own sense of design and significance.

We should also observe that Thoreau's resistance to the influence of the market is not limited to the economic sphere in this more literal sense but extends to a number of other kinds of influence. For instance, although he worked actively for the abolition of slavery, championed John Brown after the attack at Harpers Ferry, and assisted men and women fleeing slavery on the "underground railroad," Thoreau refused to join any abolitionist society. The rationale for such avoidance is again a perspicuity about individual responsibility and a distrust of joint ventures in which the will of the many can influence the conscience of the one. For Emerson, Thoreau's refusal of a position of "command" (or participation in any organization structured more rigidly than a "huckleberry party") was one of Thoreau's failings. And we might think that his refusals are finally, as we say, "self-defeating."

In an influential (if now somewhat dated) interpretation of the literature of the American Renaissance, Richard Poirier reads the refusal of writers to accede to the orders imposed by the market, political or religious orthodoxy, or other schemes of will and belief in relation to a phrase used by the Roman General Coriolanus, in Shakespeare's play of that title, as seeking "a world elsewhere" (*Coriolanus* 3.3.135). For Poirier, these writers react to their cultural milieu by attempting to create a virtual alternative, a purer and more ideal community of mind, through verbal means, over against the sordid and striving society they perceive around them. As he puts it, writers such as Thoreau respond as if to the feeling that "there is nothing in the real world, or in the systems which dominate it, that can possibly satisfy their aspirations" (Poirier 5). Their efforts therefore are aimed at creating through language "environments radically different from those supported by economic, political, or social systems," though "the enormous contrivances of language called forth by this effort are themselves an admission the environment thus created has an existence only in style" (16-17). The result, he says, is "an aesthetic so devoted to the activity of creation that it denies finality to the results of that activity, its objects or formulations. Art is an action not a product of action" (21). A corollary result of this orientation is writing that is "a kind of drama of the search for clarity" (ix). In a very important way, as we will see in the next chapter, Thoreau does deny finality to any act of creation, though he seems far less persuaded of the "reality" of the "systems that dominate" the supposed real world of social circumstance than do others—notably Emerson. By that I mean he is more certain than most that such systems are local and specific products, perhaps approximating a deeper or higher truth (and certain to have actual effects, as both truths and fictions may) but never quite attaining the condition of truth themselves. Our own formulations seem not quite to encapsulate Thoreau's intentions, and this one no less than all the rest. Poirier's formulation applies aptly to the case of Thoreau by marking the resistance to imposed orders and the tentativeness or transience of oppositional stances suggested by his work. It fails to apply only in that Thoreau seems to have consistently retained faith in a real world that exceeds our currently cowed aspirations and to have persistently remained open to the possibility that beyond what he had written or thought there was in fact "more day to dawn" (223).

18

Discussion Questions

1. Consider Thoreau's idea of "community" in further detail. How do his statements about community compare with the idea of Thoreau as an individualist? In what ways does his idea of community seem common or uncommon?

2. What is Emerson's chief complaint about Thoreau in his eulogy for him? What does this suggest about the differences between the two writers?

3. Specify an example of "thought" or writing that is "sponsored" in the sense meant in this chapter. What is apparently wrong with this kind of sponsoring from Thoreau's point of view?

4. What does Thoreau's emphasis on his own autonomy and freedom of thought suggest about his relationship to what Poirier calls "systems which dominate" the "real world"? How is Poirier's use of the phrase "real world" limited here? How does Thoreau's apparent resistance complicate or clarify the possible meanings of "community" in his writing?

2

Walden

An Experiment in Thinking on Location

> "We commonly do not remember that it is, after all, always the first person that is speaking."— *Walden* (1)

Thoreau began writing *Walden* in 1846 and continued working on it through seven distinct revisions until it was published in 1854. That decade saw the publication also of the most memorable of the works of those writers identified with the American Renaissance. Among them, to cite only the most famous, were *The Scarlet Letter*, *Moby-Dick*, *Uncle Tom's Cabin*, and *Leaves of Grass*. Among the writers closely identified with the first stage of this renaissance, only Emerson and Poe (who died in 1849) had published significantly earlier than these canonical writers. Emerson's book-length essay *Nature* had appeared in 1836, his *Essays: First Series* in 1841, *Essays: Second Series* in 1844, *Nature; Addresses and Lectures* in 1849, and *Representative Men* in 1850. Popular works of the day included travel books or "excursions" which Thoreau read omnivorously and which Melville's early novels mimicked in form and content while he claimed considerable and increasing latitude in turning them into narratives that also incorporated philosophical reflection.

Ostensibly a narrative about an experiment of living in the woods, *Walden* casts a glance at excursion narratives when Thoreau's narrator says in its early pages: "I would fain say something, not so much concerning the Chinese and Sandwich Islanders as you who read these pages, who are said to live in New England..."(2). So saying, he appears to mix assumptions about genres at the same time that he specifies a relatively narrow and immediate audience. Wordplay is, of course, immediately evident in the New England colloquialisms "not so much" (more than a synonym for "not at all," it implies "but possibly somewhat") and "fain" ("be eager," but also a homonym for "feign" = "make a pretence"), and the phrase "said to live" (questioning what one means by "live"). The voice of this narrative alternates between intense sincerity and both pointed and guarded irony, but even to rely too strongly on these terms is to accept unwittingly an opposition the voice itself contests—as if one could not be both sincere and ironic.

Traditional forms of European philosophical discourse typically perform their work within relatively narrow generic bounds—those of the apology, epistle, dialogue, or treatise—in which an audience is invoked to share the concerns and assumptions of the principal speaker or author of the work. Beginning with an explanation of his purpose, and invoking an audience, Thoreau's narrator states a reason for intruding his affairs on the attention of others. Yet intentions seem to multiply and layer themselves in the turns of phrase and ambiguities of words, as if to insist that one listen closely to exactly what is being said. Traditionally, philosophers begin with the assumption that words or names have (or can have) clear and proper significations, that language itself presumes an order of things or of thought (or both), so that reasoning can arrive at conclusions or answers through verbal or symbolic means alone. Where these assumptions seem to be inadequate, philosophers tend to adopt one of two remedial strategies: either (1) to attempt to purge language of its accreted, wayward meanings and cant (language used to deceive and obscure) by recalling root meanings and etymologies; or, (2) to develop new names or to substitute abstract symbols for words to attain stricter denotation. Historically, however, these strategies are so often adopted without solving the problem that language itself becomes a problem for philosophy; hence, the modern and post-modern attention given to language as a key philosophical problem or issue. To the traditional aims of philosophy, language can be seen as a perpetually re-discovered stumbling block, because it manifests itself as a phenomenon (or set of phenomena) to be explained and because it is never as stable as a search for timeless truth would require. But having set out with somewhat different expectations about the model of philosophy to be pursued, Thoreau's use of parable and wordplay turns a roadblock into a pathway. Rather than resisting the tendency of words meant in one sense to recall those meant in another, to slip toward them in meaning, Thoreau exploits these phenomena as a resource for thinking. He celebrates allusiveness and polysemy. Indeed, he often even takes the purely verbal metonymy of the pun as a hinge to connect disparate signifiers, as though the surface connection of sound signifies a deeper or more transcendent one of thought or reality.

Thoreau's always complex voicing of his utterances can be contrasted starkly with the early aspirations of transcendentalist writing and compared as closer in kind to the meditations of a fiction writer such as Melville. For American Transcendentalism begins not in the mode of crisis but in an almost sublime (some have thought ridiculous) state of innocence and indifference to problems existing in philosophy for some time. In his early essay *Nature* (1836), for instance, Emerson announces:

> Undoubtedly we have no questions to ask which are unanswerable. We must trust to the perfection of creation so far, as to believe that whatever curiosity the order of things has awakened in our minds, the order of things can satisfy. Every man's condition is a solution in hieroglyphic to those inquiries he would put. He acts it as life, before he apprehends it as truth. (*Essays and Lectures* 7)

Live simply and sincerely enough and the truth will be revealed; avoid the sins of the fathers, recorded in their books, and all things will become new—and more: "whenever a true theory appears, it will be its own evidence" (7)—for symbol and thought are iconicly related. So Emerson seems to say, but much of the drama of reading through Emerson's essays in sequence comes from seeing him grapple with the complications and frayings of these initial, simple assumptions— almost childlike in their simplicity and their resistance to the awareness of history. In contrast, Thoreau seems to begin with the assumption that truth is more complex and elusive (he uses the word "volatile" [*Walden* 217]), requiring suppler uses of language and vision, as in the following passage from the chapter "The Pond in

Winter" which seems to answer back to such an assertion as Emerson's:

> After a still winter night I awoke with the impression that some question had been put to me, which I had been endeavoring in vain to answer in my sleep, as what—how—when—where? But there was dawning nature, in whom all creatures live, looking in at my broad windows with serene and satisfied face, and no question on *her* lips. I awoke to an unanswered question, to Nature and daylight. The snow lying deep on the earth dotted with young pines, and the very slope of the hill on which my house is placed, seemed to say, Forward! Nature puts no question and answers none which we mortals ask. She has long ago taken her resolution. "O Prince, our eyes contemplate with admiration and transmit to the soul the wonderful and varied spectacle of this universe. The night veils without doubt part of this glorious creation; but day comes to reveal to us this great work, which extends from earth even into the plains of the ether." (188)

This curiously opaque passage suggests where philosophy might begin or begin again for the individual—in an unanswered question and a sense of wonder—but explicitly denies that Nature puts forward the questions we ask. These questions, the passage seems to imply, are ours alone. Nature reveals different aspects of "her" self (thus personified) but not *our*selves, which we might infer are revealed instead in our strivings. Quoting from a Sanskrit text he had translated from a French translation, the *Harivansa*, Thoreau suggests moreover that one revelation both obscures and supersedes another, but not without skirting this irony: The day also obscures what the night reveals, as the sun's light hides the light of the stars. Irony thus is not inconsistent with the pursuit of true expression in Thoreau's vision, nor is an "unanswered question" inconsistent with our life in nature.

As if in response to his own question "Why do precisely these objects which we behold make a world?" (*Walden* 150), Thoreau appears to assume that "these objects" do indeed "make a world." At the same time, he seems content with and even to celebrate the appearance of difference that gives rise to the question, as though the sense of wonder emerges from the discrepancy between faith in unity and the appearance of multiplicity as both an aesthetic and cognitive stimulus. Given his eventual development toward the practice of natural science, it is worth noting here his resolution of this problem in the adoption of philosophical perspectivism in *Walden*:

If we knew all the laws of Nature, we should need only one fact, or the description of one actual phenomenon, to infer all the particular results at that point. Now we know only a few laws, and our result is vitiated, not, of course, by any confusion or irregularity in Nature, but in our ignorance of essential elements in the calculation. Our notions of law and harmony are commonly confined to those instances which we detect; but the harmony which results from a far greater number of seemingly conflicting, but really concurring, laws, which we have not detected, is still more wonderful. The particular laws are as our points of view, as, to the traveller [sic], a mountain outline varies with every step, and it has an infinite number of profiles, though absolutely but one form. Even when cleft or bored through it is not comprehended in its entireness. (194)

The unity of the laws of nature as manifested in "one fact" or "the description of one actual phenomenon" is axiomatic: "Nature" is what we mean by this unity. We assume such unity exists because it makes more rather than less sense to do so. One might call the approach either pragmatic or idealistic without getting any closer to or further away from the truth of the matter, for it is consistent with either orientation. Moreover, in setting these premises, not as a ground-clearing exercise at the beginning of his discourse but as yet another observation in the midst of his narrative of habitation, it is as though Thoreau's narrator were trying to describe how consciousness situates or locates itself with respect to Nature, which it is *in* but not *of*, in order to describe relationships between consciousness and nature, consciousness and other consciousness, and consciousness and itself. In sum, he might agree with Wittgenstein that "The world is all that is the case" (*Tractatus* 1) and "The feeling of the world as a bounded thing is a mystical feeling" (*Tractatus* 6.45).

Getting Down to Cases

Central themes of *Walden*, then, are the relations of human beings to nature, to each other, and to themselves. It would be hard to be more comprehensive in scope in a narrative that centers on the stay of a little over two years at a New England pond, geologically remarkable for being a "kettle hole," or deep body of inland water without surface inlet or outlet. Thoreau makes that centering itself a theme by emphasizing the need for anyone—writer or thinker or "poor student" to whom the work is partly addressed—to begin where he or she is. By a perspective making relativism he shares with the Emerson of "The American Scholar," he denies the presumed privilege of traditional locations for the advancement of knowledge. As Emerson writes, "meek young men grow up in libraries, believing it the duty to accept the views, which Cicero, which Locke, which Bacon, have given, forgetful that Cicero, Locke, and Bacon were only young men in libraries" (*Essays and Lectures* 57). Removed from the scene of the library, the pond becomes the site for contemplation and writing, recalling for Thoreau perhaps (among other things) "the borders of the lake" to which Vibhradja "betook himself" in the *Harivansa*, and where other characters "recalling to mind the borders of the sacred lake, recovered at the same time their ancient sentiments of devotion" (*Transmigration of the Seven Brahmans* 8, 13).

Mixing precept with anecdote and parable in the manner of such narratives, *Walden* poses some problems for students and critics regarding how we may sort out the relationships between those precepts and bring the whole into a more confirmed sequential and hierarchical order than appears to be given. One could complain of that mixing as E.B. White did when he compared the book to an omelet and asserted that Thoreau wrote "very likely without knowing quite what he was up to" ("Walden—1954" 360). Yet subsequent criticism has revealed the long process of composition and revision of the book through at least seven distinct versions. Throughout these stages, the seasonal structure (from summer to fall, winter to spring) and dialectical pattern of the arrangement of chapters (as though one implicitly comments on another) emerges, suggesting that Thoreau wrote as deliberately as he claimed he desired to live while at the pond. Alternations of time, tense, and mood, of abstract and actual, in his writing have the consequence of imitating the movements of thought and attention in daily life and providing a phenomenological authenticity to the whole.

A certain doubleness of voice we have already noted informs this work, as well as a habit of thinking that one position or set of circumstances implies others equally as real. Indeed, doubleness or multiplicity can be said to reflect the epistemological condition and insight out of which the book is written without causing Thoreau to deny the relevance of terms like "truth":

No face which we can give to a matter will stead us so well at last as the truth. For the most part, we are not where we are, but in a false position. Through an infirmity of our natures, we suppose a case, and put ourselves into it, and hence are in two cases at the same time, and it is doubly difficult to get out. (*Walden* 219)

"To get out" here appears to signify the condition of achieving clarity (as Poirier suggests in his critique) outside the bounds imposed by our own descriptions. This passage is nicely characteristic of Thoreau, embedding a simple statement of an epistemological dilemma in metaphors of surveying, social relations, and formal debate in the phrase "false position." It articulates a commonly experienced dilemma: How do we know where we are, and in relation to what? Which of two cases present to the mind is the "correct" one? How do we decide? If we do not know where we are, how do we know what or who we are? What, outside of ourselves, admittedly already finding ourselves dis-oriented, will provide us with an orientation?

These questions are such as inspired Emerson's long meditation in the essay "Experience" (published in *Essays: Second Series* in 1844), Melville's mediations by proxy in *Moby-Dick* (1851), and more distantly in Puritan or Calvinist dramas of spiritual debate, of which William Cowper's "The Cast-Away" (1799) will be mentioned here. By citing this range of texts, I want to suggest that Thoreau's concern with an epistemological dilemma extends to ethical and spiritual dimensions at the same time that his language enables us to imagine it in other lived contexts such as the embarrassment of a "false position" socially or romantically, or in an intellectual debate; or the peril or fatality of a "false position" in exploration or navigation. What I will call his depiction of the "Dilemma of Two Cases" describes a form of consciousness that can have a number of different kinds of content but is always felt keenly in the conflict of imperatives or judgments. "What shall I do?" cries Bunyan's Christian, *in* the world but not *of* it (*Pilgrim's Progress* 3). The dilemma of consciousness, which I would argue is just what Thoreau explores in *Walden*, is similar.

The Spectator, the Self and the Dilemma of Consciousness

Both Thoreau's narrator in *Walden* and Melville's narrator Ishmael in *Moby-Dick* go into solitude in response to pressures in their environments in a manner common to romantic narrators and a whole line of melancholy malcontents before them. Ishmael pronounces his taking to the sea as his substitute for "the cap and ball"—suicide or murderous mayhem. Thoreau prefaces the narrative proper of *Walden* with an epigraph that tells us that he does not propose "to write an ode to dejection" (an allusion to Coleridge's "Dejection: An Ode" and other poems in that genre) but "to brag as lustily as chanticleer...." Despite that disclaimer, however, Thoreau's narrator tells a tale about actions that are clearly at odds with the expectations of members of his audience. His excuse for telling about himself is specifically that people have asked about his unexplained (or inexplicable) actions. Both Ishmael and the narrator of *Walden* tell of seeking a re-orientation in which a problem of consciousness—the alternation of mood between sociability and irritability, and perhaps irritability resulting from sociability—plays a part and motivates the first-person narrator's actions. Thoreau's narrator complains of the conditions and expectations of life in society, leading him to the subsequent forthright assertion:

> I went to the woods because I wished to live deliberately, to front only the essential facts of life, and see if I could not learn what it had to teach, and not, when I came to die, discover that I had not lived. I did not wish to live what was not life.... (61)

Literal-minded mockers have responded to the heroic diction of this passage by pointing out that Walden Pond was not *that* far into the woods even in 1846 and so have lost (and lose) the sense of the narrative. (In fact, I am using the phrase 'Thoreau's narrator" rather than "Thoreau" to keep us from too simple a biographical analysis.) The implication of the words is clear, as far as the narrator is concerned: To live in society is not "to live deliberately," not "to front...the essential facts of life" and in short "to live what [is] not life." This is not to say that "Thoreau" makes these assertions as universally true, but rather true for that "Thoreau" who appears as narrator, and who is eventually construed as one of the avatars of a historical Thoreau who also had "several more lives to live" (215). The point of these acts of radical reorientation—actual and fictive at once—is to develop a perspective on our presumed knowledge by the continual examination of the notion of position within circumstances or "cases." Thoreau's narrator positions himself at extremes or margins of "normal" experience, as for instance when the passage quoted above continues:

27

I wanted to live deep and suck out all the marrow of life; to live
so sturdily and Spartan-like as to put to rout all that was not life,
to cut a broad swath and shave close, to drive life into a corner,
and reduce it to its lowest terms, and, if it proved to be mean, why
then to get the whole and genuine meanness of it, and publish its
meanness to the world; or if it were sublime, to know it by
experience, and be able to give a true account of it in my next
excursion. (61)

"In my next excursion" implies "not in this one" where he seems
intent on overturning the self-satisfaction of people with what they
presume to be the case. Yet this dispute with superficial knowledge
never comes so close to a literal denial as to be cowed by a lack of
resolution of the question (is life mean or is it sublime?) which would
require another, more comprehensive and totalizing, summation of
what is the case: "For most men, it appears to me, are in a strange
uncertainty about it [life], whether it is of the devil or of God, and
have somewhat hastily concluded that it is the chief end of man to
'glorify God and enjoy him forever'" (61). He avoids the blasphemy
of denying the locally traditional Christian doctrine (the phrase is
quoted from the Shorter Catechism of the New England Primer), but
neither does he affirm it. The haste of most men in their conclusion
stems from their experiential uncertainty, which ought to keep the
question open for them since it does not confirm, by experience, the
truth of their words. Rhetorically, it incites the thinker not to stop with
the inherited form of words but to try them experientially or (as the
close connection between the words suggests) experimentally. Here as
elsewhere, however, both what we experience as mean and what we
experience as sublime are, as it were, contained within experience. So
they are, like views of the mountain, relative and consequent to our
positions in experience, parts of but not the whole truth we might
pursue.

    Further on, Thoreau's narrator expresses again this dilemma of
consciousness *in* but not *of* Nature, when he asserts that:

With thinking we may be beside ourselves in a sane sense. By a
conscious effort of the mind we can stand aloof from actions and
their consequences; and all things, good and bad, go by us like a
torrent. We are not wholly involved in Nature. I may be either
driftwood in the stream, or Indra in the sky looking down on it. I
may be affected by a theatrical exhibition; on the other hand, I

may not be affected by an actual event which appears to concern me much more. I only know myself as a human entity, the scene so to speak, of thoughts and affections; and am sensible of a certain doubleness by which I stand as remote from myself as from another. However intense my experience, I am conscious of the presence and criticism of a part of me, which, as it were, is not part of me, but spectator, sharing no experience, but taking note of it. When the play, it may be the tragedy, of life is over, the spectator goes his way. It was a kind of fiction, a work of the imagination only, so far as he was concerned. This doubleness may make us poor neighbors and friends sometimes. (91)

The transition from a vision recalling Arjuna's in the *Bhagavad Gita* (i.e., 13.13-17; Radhakrishnan 146) to mundane observations about neighborliness is a rapid descent. "The spectator goes his way," apparently disembodied. But what way and where? Is it a consolation that the life whose "essential facts" one had tried "to front" may be a "kind of fiction, a work of the imagination only," and that knowledge can thus be disembodied? Which of two "cases" or frames of reference—that of "driftwood in the stream" or "Indra in the sky," abject and sublime—will hold? Or so we might ask only to discover that we are asking experientially based questions about something that is not experiential but transcendent.

The theatrical metaphor employed by Thoreau might suggest to us as well that he is recalling not only the *Bhagavad Gita* but also Hume's reflections on "personal identity" in *A Treatise of Human Nature* (Book I, Part IV, Section VI). Like Hume, Thoreau does not accept the notion that we have a self such "that we feel its existence and its continuance in existence; and are certain, beyond the evidence of a demonstration, both of its perfect identity and simplicity" (Hume 251). The "spectator," when it goes its way, may go to oblivion. There is no metaphysical identity that supersedes existence, and "self or person is not any one impression, but that to which our several impressions and ideas are suppos'd to have reference" (Hume 251). Hence Thoreau's patience with metaphorical terms such as "kind of fiction" and "work of imagination" in characterizing the experience of the "human entity." Like Hume, too, he would, if systematically inclined, distinguish between "personal identity as regards our thought and imagination, and as it regards our passions or the concern we take in ourselves" (Hume 253), because it is precisely in confusing the two that we conflate feeling with a transcendental object or form.

29

Participating in experience as subjects, acting as agents, and observing both the participation and the action, "we are not where we are" through the complexity of locating ourselves and through "an infirmity of our natures" which we call consciousness. Among other things, we must be "beside ourselves," albeit "in a sane sense," in thought because that is principally what "thought" means. The experience of the "human entity" is the alternation between the experience of selflessness and self-presence, immersion in experience and awareness of the presence and criticism of the spectator-self "taking note" of that experience. Thus, Thoreau's depiction, through his narrator, of experiences that we might call mystical are explicable, as in the oft-quoted passage regarding his hoeing beans:

> When my hoe tinkled against the stone, that music echoed to the woods and the sky, and was an accompaniment to my labor which yielded an instant and immeasurable crop. It was no longer beans that I hoed, nor I that hoed beans; and I remembered with as much pity as pride, my acquaintances who had gone to the city to attend oratorios. (107)

Or in another moment of selflessness:

> Sometimes I watched a pair of hen-hawks circling the sky, alternately soaring and descending, approaching and leaving one another, as if they were the imbodiment [sic] of my own thoughts. (107)

It is important to understand that these are neither merely metaphorical embellishments nor assertions of access to some other mode of being than is available to other human entities. They are phenomenologically accurate descriptions of states of consciousness which may be rare or extreme in most people's daily experience but which nevertheless do exist. They describe moments in which the spectator views the experience of the self or ego (as agent) when the boundaries between self or ego and its objects have broken down— "no longer beans that I hoed nor I that hoed beans." One could say that they thus also describe one polarity of consciousness, a boundary experience that is close to the limit of what we call living by which we know how we are limited or, in Thoreau's phrase, "yarded" (216).

The split between spectator and self-as-agent is not unlike that between different persons, giving rise to Thoreau's use of personification in describing the spectator as distinct from the self, so that the subject is "beside" itself "in a sane sense." And perhaps the only way we understand such splits within ourselves is, paradoxically, as a cohabitation of two selves or two minds. The two paragraphs following the opening of "The Pond in Winter" (a passage we considered above) move from a description of the self in the world to a consideration of the self in relation to other selves in a series of transitions that warrant quoting at length:

> Then to my morning work. First I take an axe and pail and go in search of water, if that be not a dream. After a cold and snowy night it needed a divining rod to find it. Every winter the liquid and trembling surface of the pond, which was so sensitive to every breath, and reflected every light and shadow, becomes solid to the depth of a foot or a foot and a half, so that it will support the heaviest teams, and perchance the snow covers it to an equal depth, and it is not to be distinguished from any level field. Like the marmots in the surrounding fields, it closes its eye-lids and becomes dormant for three months or more. Standing on the snow-covered plain, as if in a pasture amid the hills, I cut my way first through a foot of snow, and then a foot of ice, and open a window under my feet, where, kneeling to drink, I look down into the quiet parlor of fishes, pervaded by a softened light as through a window of ground glass, with its bright sanded floor the same as in summer; there a perennial waveless serenity as in the amber twilight sky, corresponding to the cool and even temperature of its inhabitants. Heaven is under our feet as well as over our heads.
>
> Early in the morning, while all things are crisp with frost, men come with fishing reels and slender lunch, and let down their fine lines through the snowy field to take pickerel and perch; wild men, who instinctively follow other fashions and trust other authorities than their townsmen, and by their comings and goings stitch towns together in parts where else they would be ripped. They sit and eat their luncheon in stout fear-naughts on the dry oak leaves on the shore, as wise in natural lore as the citizen is in artificial. They never consulted with books, and know and can tell much less than they have done. The things they practise [sic] are said not yet to be known. Here is one fishing for pickerel with perch for bait. You look into his pail with wonder as into a summer pond, as if he kept summer locked up at home, or knew

where she had retreated. How, pray, did he get these in mid-winter? O, he got worms out of rotten logs since the ground froze, and so he caught them. His life passes deeper in Nature that the studies of the naturalist penetrate; himself a subject for the naturalist. The latter raise the moss and bark gently with his knife in search of insects; the former lays open logs to their core with his axe, and moss and bark fly far and wide. He gets his living by barking trees. Such as man has some right to fish, and I love to see Nature carried out in him. The perch swallows the grub-worm, the pickerel swallows the perch, and the fisherman swallows the pickerel; and so all the chinks in the scale of being are filled. (188-189)

Compared to the workings of ordinary philosophy, these paragraphs are extraordinary in the kinds of "knowledge" they allow to pass by as well as in what they apprehend. Rather than seeking certainty about the reality of his perceptions ("if that be not a dream"), the narrator is content to describe them in the present tense (making the experience immediate and progressive, not distant and completed). Consequently, the self that is the narrator and the self that is narrated are not abstracted from experience; and neither, to the extent that he or she participates in the narration, is the reader. None has an existence coincident with the other in a literal sense (the self that narrates has gone its way; the self that is narrated likewise is "gone"; and the reader exists at some point in a present which belongs to neither), yet each is nominated in the persisting discourse as a possibility of existence. The narrator lets the famous problem of distinguishing between dream and "reality" go by with a mere mention.

A number of orientational metaphors in this passage stand, as it were, our assumptions about ordinary experience on their head. The horizontal ice becomes a typically vertical "window" exposing a timeless scene like in its qualities to a still "twilight sky," leading to the final inversion: "Heaven is under our feet as well as over our heads." One could say that this is mere wordplay. But what is the point of the play? One thinks, we might paraphrase, that our experience is solid and our distinctions between inner and out, upper and lower, summer and winter, heaven and earth are clear; but experience teaches us otherwise. Experience will not confirm all of our verbal formulations arising from particular "cases" or circumstances and being transposed to another. Experience, rather, teaches us that transposition is more often the case; ordinary assumptions about ordinary experience, articulated in language, only serve to deliver us to the extraordinary. Even the confusion of "reality" for a "dream"—a staple problem for philosophical reflection—is controverted, for a dream is reality and reality is not to be equated with our common assumptions. Look under the ice and one finds the semblance of summer, and, further, look to the untutored and find that they know how to import summer into winter in a pail.

The "wild men" depicted in the second of these paragraphs represent a polarity in the narrator's thinking to the spectator self, for they are the ones observed, yet never penetrated: "his life passes deeper in Nature than the studies of the naturalist penetrate; himself a subject for the naturalist." To paraphrase again, the narrator implies that the function of the naturalist is to describe phenomena of nature rather than to "carry out" Nature in his actions. The "wild men" act from instinct, have never "consulted with books," and the "things which they practise [sic] are said not yet to be known," even though by their commerce they "stitch towns together" (i.e. extend the community) in desolate places where communities do not customarily have contact with each other. In terms of contemporary critical analysis, they might be referred to as liminal figures who exist on the borders of the community and of nature, even of thought, and function in the discourse of the supposedly learned both to mark and to cover over the difference between these domains. They are, distantly, in the human community but not of it, as the narrator (and reader) is in but not of its opposite (here at least) "Nature." As such they appear as opposites to what he calls "the spectator," which is also a liminal concept mediating between lived experience and the unlived totality (or what Wittgenstein might have called the negative truth) of possibility for the individual.

These passages do not, of course, represent a philosophical argument for a particular or general "case" or "state of affairs"; they do not issue in propositions that can be built upon to construct a field of thought. The lack of consecutive argument does not mean that Thoreau is incapable of sequential, logical inference as we might infer if we read *Walden* alone. Rather, this mode of discourse disputes in its practice the idea that we can arrive at ultimate and timeless propositional knowledge of the nature of ourselves or the nature of nature by inference—or that such "knowledge" would be useful. It does so without disputing that there is a state of affairs, a set of "cases," which we may not imagine, and indeed it includes the premise that there is always somewhat outside of our experience and beside ourselves that we have not apprehended. That is the point of the allegory of the mountain. It is itself a field in which the play of thought (language) is sensible insofar as it makes sense and where the appropriate audience is one that has "ears to hear." In it, the dilemma of consciousness is the dilemma in which we live and move and have our being—where we have such commerce as we have with others and with the world.

Two Illuminating Cases: Cowper and Melville

By way of contextualizing Thoreau's project involving the dilemma of consciousness, I mentioned two other writers and texts, in addition to Emerson and his writing, which I would like to consider briefly as illuminating cases by comparison, before turning to take a final look at what Thoreau says about his own medium—language—in *Walden*. Cowper and Melville help to establish a context for understanding Thoreau in relation to the Puritan tradition. Puritan and Calvinist (and much other) religious thought entails dilemmas of knowledge and will that can be simply stated:

1. The ultimate disposition of my soul, eternally existing, whether of salvation of damnation, is of the utmost importance to me; yet I can have no direct knowledge of it. Even inferences about it may be deceiving, and make me conceive of myself as either saved or damned against what is the case, except God's grace reveal it to me, and of such grace I may have only a conviction and not certain knowledge.
2. The thing I would most desire, my salvation, is beyond my power, so that whatever I will is naught; if I will other than my salvation I am lost certainly, yet I can bring myself no closer to salvation by my will.

This what the Christian, in this meaning of the term, means by "original sin," that he or she is in a "false position" by virtue of existing and that the false position can only be made true by God's grace, which is particular to each person. Thus, the Christian in this sense believes that he or she lives divided between a sinful and mortal self and a soul that is eternal and may or may not be subject to God's particular grace. In contrast to the sort of generalized salvation that many people who think of themselves as (at least nominally) Christian may believe in, such a notion of salvation is personal and particular.

Within this worldview, God provides grace or acts providentially with respect to a hierarchy of concerns. As one English Puritan, John Beadle, wrote in the mid-seventeenth century:

> Some acts of God, are acts of common providence, and so he feeds us, and cloaths [sic] us, he doth as much for the creatures; so he feeds the Ravens....Some acts of God are acts of speciall [sic] privilege; and thus he gave Abraham a child in his old age, and made David of a Shepherd a King. Some acts of God, are acts of pattern; and thus he showed mercy to Menasse....Some acts of God are acts of wonder: it is a wonder that any man is saved. (Beadle 59-60).

Each word of the concluding sentence is meant emphatically. Within a general framework of providential design, these levels are discrete. God feeds and clothes us, but he does as much for the ravenous birds; he acts according to a pattern that can be discerned in history, discontinuous as history may seem; but the one thing that is most needed is an "act of wonder," meaning an event that cannot be predicted, explained, or otherwise determined by reference to objective conditions or facts.

For any such believers, consideration of the state of the soul is a matter of life and death, and there is no absolute certainty to be had regarding it. One is admittedly in a false position; there is no way out by one's own efforts. The dilemma of such a consciousness is played out in a remarkable poem, "The Cast-Away" (1799) by the 18th century British poet William Cowper, best known as author of the hymn "God moves in a mysterious way." Cowper believed that he was damned in a way that modern psychologists would call pathological. He did not disbelieve in God or in the doctrines of salvation and God's grace. Indeed, he touchingly and devoutly wrote of such in a series of hymns of praise and wonder. He simply believed that he was damned. No evidence to the contrary could matter, since evidence could always be false. As others had the conviction of salvation, he had the opposite. He had the conviction of damnation.

The poem tells the story, based on an historical incident, of a man who falls overboard from a ship in a storm. His mates, despite their efforts, cannot turn against the storm, and he struggles:

> Nor soon he felt his strength decline
>   Or courage die away;

But waged with Death a lasting strife
Supported by despair of life.

Although he is abandoned, he does not blame them:

Yet bitter felt it still to die
Deserted, and his friends so nigh.

Then the last two of eleven short stanzas turn toward the lyrical application of this emblematic story:

I, therefore, purpose not or dream,
    Descanting on his fate,
To give the melancholy theme
    A more enduring date,
But mis'ry still delights to trace
Its semblance in anothers' [sic] case.

No voice divine the storm allay'd,
    No light propitious shone,
When, snatch'd from all effectual aid,
    We perish'd, each, alone;
But I, beneath a rougher sea,
And whelm'd in deeper gulphs than he.

Like most of Cowper's poems, this one is notable for the balance and restraint, even delicacy, of its language in treating matters that do not typically inspire tact. The unnamed cause of the speaker's sinking, and he speaks to the reader after he is "whelm'd," is only by implication spiritual or psychological, but few readers will take it otherwise. For those who lack a comparable conviction of the reality of sin, it will appear that speaker imagines himself falsely, or they will psychologize his despair. In doing the latter, however, they will find this state of mind to be a false one, such "gulphs" the result of a supposition of the mind contrary to fact. Yet these readers will also recognize that such beliefs have real effects and such imaginings may act on the mind like real existences.

The poem represents a form of belief alive within Thoreau's time and culture (as we will see by Melville's reference to the poem) which surely speaks to the matter of "quiet desperation" and the sustaining desire to "front" life and know whether it is sublime or mean, of God or the devil. And it speaks as well to the gulf between "human entities" who, whatever else they do, do "perish[...], each, alone." But it represents as well a characteristic dilemma of consciousness. For to suppose ourselves in this position, in death-in-life, like the speaker of the poem, is not to "brag as lustily as chanticleer," and not to be in a state of conviviality, though we cannot at the same time fully deny the proposition that "we die alone." A living man who writes a poem such as "The Cast-Away" must be in a "false position" in one sense or another, since he has not literally drowned, and yet perhaps also in a true one representing his state of mind. So paradox or irony inhibits our use of language to say we are one thing only and not another, and thought, which is always in Thoreau's sense an act of supposition, places us at once in a false position and in the only position we can have as human entities. To throw oneself into a conviction about the state of one's soul is, from the point of view Thoreau offers, to mistake the feeling one has about oneself for a belief in something metaphysical. In Hume's words, it is to confuse "that to which our several impressions and ideas are supposed to have reference" for something of which we "are certain, beyond the evidence of a demonstration, both of its perfect identity and simplicity." We would be mistaken to think, I would argue, that Thoreau has the same idea of self that Cowper has, of that kind of personal identity, and to read him as suggesting such.

Thoreau, of course, did not invent the idea that personal identity and the life it has reference to is "a kind of fiction, a work of the imagination only," whatever the nature of "the spectator." Nor did he invent irony and paradox and the sense of complication that arises from observing that contrary cases may be true in the world without leading to despair. As an example contemporary to Thoreau, we might consider Melville's meditations through his narrator Ishmael in *Moby-Dick*. In Chapter 93 of that novel, titled "The Castaway," Ishmael tells the story of the abandonment of Pip, a small black ship-keeper on the whaling voyage of the *Pequod*. In telling the story, he intimates that he will also be abandoned later (in contrast to the situation in Cowper's poem, however, the narrator escapes and the rest of the crew drowns). But here the focus is on Pip and his circumstances.

The story concerns, at a practical level, the inadequacy of universal propositions or rules applied to existential situations. Pip has once jumped overboard from the whaleboat and become entangled in the harpoon-line fastened to a whale so that the mate Stubb has had to cut loose the whale to save the boy. After Pip is assailed by the rest of the crew for his action:

> Stubb then in a plain, business-like, but still half humorous manner, cursed Pip officially; and that done, unofficially gave him much wholesome advice. The substance was, Never jump from the boat, Pip, except—but all the rest was indefinite, as the soundest advice ever is. Now, in general, Stick to the boat, is your true motto in whaling; but cases will sometimes happen when Leap from the boat, is still better. Moreover, as if perceiving that if he should give undiluted conscientious advice to leave him too wide a margin to jump in the future; Stubb suddenly dropped all advice, and concluded with a peremptory command, "Stick to the boat, Pip, or by the Lord, I wont pick you up if you jump; mind that." (*Moby-Dick* 413)

The sense conveyed by this passage, as by many others in the novel, is of a world in which contrary propositions can as likely be equally true as not, or at least fail in their predictive power consistently enough to complicate rule-making. Stubbs solution is to stick with the rule that is marginally more certain than the other, and in any case to choose, as Ishmael notes, not the rule that will protect Pip best but the command that agrees most with the object of whaling, to make money: "We can't afford to lose whales by the likes of you; a whale would sell for thirty times what you would, Pip, in Alabama" (413). But Pip does jump from the boat on a subsequent occasion, and he is left behind but later rescued, becoming an "idiot" from the shock of his experience:

> The sea had jeeringly kept his finite body up, but drowned the infinite of his soul. Not drowned entirely though. Rather carried down alive to wondrous depths, where strange shapes of the unwarped primal world glided to and fro before his passive eyes; and the miser-merman, Wisdom, revealed his hoarded heaps; and among the joyous, heartless, ever-juvenile eternities, Pip saw the multitudinous, God-omnipresent, coral insects, that out of the firmament of waters heaved colossal orbs. He saw God's foot upon the treadle of the loom, and spoke it; and therefore his shipmates called him mad. So man's insanity is heaven's sense; and wandering from all mortal reason, man comes at last to that celestial thought, which, to reason, is absurd and frantic; and weal or woe, feels then uncompromised, indifferent as his God. (414)

Pip's encounter with extreme or primal Nature leads him (in Ishmael's imagining) to a place of "joyous, heartless, ever-juvenile eternities," incorporating contraries and transcending them, and thereby vacating the place of what is normally called "reason." And while this is a more extreme picture of nature than we commonly expect from Thoreau, it results in inversions that we typically do expect from him. Moreover, it results in Pip's liberation from the tyranny of reason, so that he feels "weal or woe, uncompromised, indifferent as his God."

To imagine contrary cases, and to act on the supposition that different cases will present themselves, is both necessary to practical life and ultimately misleading and mind-entangling when it comes to considering the world as a transcendent horizon of our knowledge. Our language is inadequate to the totality of what is the case, because we can always only suppose through the "rational," non-paradoxical, and un-ironic use of language cases less complex than the world turns out to be. The alternative in Ishmael's world, for those "not drowned entirely" who escape to tell of the experience of crossing boundaries of sense, is emblematized by the "devious cruising" of the ship *Rachel* that seeking to find several lost souls (including the captain's son) finds and saves him instead: an event whose irony can be chalked up equally to wondrous providence or mere chance. Another way of expressing what is emblematized by the figure of the ship would be to borrow from navigation and call it "triangulation." For both Melville and Thoreau, who borrows his metaphors from the parallel craft of surveying, as we have seen, it is better to approach truth by indirection rather than by direct pursuit; those who discover are those who wander on the margins, liminal figures such as Pip and Ishmael in *Moby-Dick*, the "ice fishers" and Thoreau's narrator in *Walden*, who go out the habitual ways of men by to encounter truth or fact where others remain in the common way. Again, in explaining why he left *Walden*, Thoreau's narrator says:

I left the woods for as good a reason as I went there. Perhaps it seemed to me that I had several more lives to live, and could not spare any more time for that one. It is remarkable how easily and insensibly we fall into a particular route, and make a beaten track for ourselves. I had not lived there a week before my feet wore a path from my door to the pond-side; and though it is five or six years since I trod it, it is still quite distinct. It is true, I fear that many others may have fallen into it, and so helped to keep it open. The surface of the earth is soft and impressionable by the feet of men; and so with the paths which the mind travels. How worn and dusty, then, must be the highways of the world, how deep the ruts of tradition and conformity! I did not wish to take a cabin passage, but rather to go before the mast and on the deck of the world, for there I could best see the moonlight amid the mountains. I do not wish to go below now. (*Walden* 215-16)

It is both remarkable and appropriate that Thoreau should express his past motivations in the form of a supposition—"perhaps it seemed to me"—since they have now become not present desires of the first-person but the facts of the life of another person existing at a different time and place, while of his present motivation he can speak affirmatively. This stylistic and rhetorical nuance is part of the design of the book in which the past, even that of the individual, having become fact, has paradoxically also become equivocal and open to interpretation, while the present and the future, in and toward which the individual acts and is, become the occasions and sites of the assertion of will: "I do not wish to go below now."

Concluding Walden

Walden concludes twice. First it concludes with the end of the chapter "Spring" and the end of the narrative of the sojourn at the pond: "Thus was my first year's life in the woods completed; and the second was similar to it: "I finally left Walden September 6th, 1847" (213). That simple journalistic statement subsumes a lot of experience under the figure of one year, ending thematically in Spring and with an emphasis on renewal, but literally in late Summer and the turning of the year toward Fall. Such circularity proscribes the territory that has been explored, implying that something is best left unexpressed:

At the same time that we are earnest to explore and learn all things, we require that all things be mysterious and unexplorable, that land and sea be infinitely wild, unsurveyed and unfathomed by us because unfathomable. We can never have enough of Nature. We must be refreshed by the sight of inexhaustible vigor, vast and Titanic features, the sea-coast with its wrecks, the wilderness with its living and decaying trees, the thunder cloud and the rain which lasts three weeks and produces freshets. We need to witness our own limits transgressed, and some life pasturing where we never wander. (212)

To "witness our own limits transgressed" is another figure for being beside ourselves "in a sane sense" (an action we may do, Thoreau says, "with thinking") since it involves both a spectator and a self or ego whose limits are those being transgressed. This would seem to be an odd figure for thinking, which we take to be done through language (whether informal or formal), and for a philosophical view, which for many has meant a winnowing of truth from untruth through the operations of language and the mills of logic. It may appear to be yet another inversion of what we expect, and thus of what we hold to be the truth. And, of course, it is a paradoxical utterance that can only be made in language and against the sufficiency of language. And so Thoreau's narrator complains in the "Conclusion"—the second one—about the limits of his (ours, anyone's) particular language:

> It is a ridiculous demand which England and America make, that you shall speak so that they can understand you. Neither men nor toadstools grow so. As if that were important, and there were not enough to understand you without them. As if Nature could support but one order of understandings, could not sustain birds as well as quadrapeds, flying as well as creeping things, and *hush* and *who*, which Bright [the common name for an ox] can understand, were the best English. I fear chiefly lest my expression not be *Extra- vagant* enough, may not wander far enough beyond the narrow limits of my daily experience, so as to be adequate to the truth of which I have been convinced. *Extra vagance!* It depends on how you are yarded. The migrating buffalo, which seeks new pastures in another latitude, is not extravagant like the cow which kicks over the pail, leaps the cow-yard fence, and runs after her calf, in milking time. I desire to speak somewhere *without* bounds; like a man in a waking moment, to men in their waking moments; for I am convinced that I cannot exaggerate enough even to lay the foundation of a true expression. Who that has heard a strain of music feared then lest he should speak extravagantly any more forever? In view of the future or possible, we should live quite laxly and undefined in front, our outlines dim and misty on that side; as our shadows reveal an invisible perspiration toward the sun. The volatile truth of our words should continually betray the inadequacy of the residual statement. Their truth is instantly *translated*; its literal monument alone remains. The words which express our faith and

piety are not definite; yet they are significant and fragrant like frankincense to superior natures. (216-217)

This passage itself presses against the limits of our language and comprehension as it asks us not to consider what is already within our ken, and to prove it, but to seek a mode of being that outstrips the predictive power of our local language while at the same time we "live quite laxly and undefined in front" in order to be open to new perceptions and thoughts. Aptly, he chooses the metaphor of translation, which includes not only our common sense of importing meaning from one language to another but the biblical sense of "conveyance to heaven without death" ("Enoch," *Harper's Bible Dictionary*; Genesis 5.24; Hebrews 11.5-6). The figure is both a radical and a revealing expression for the conveyance or communication of truth through language because it returns us to the mystery of acts of communication (while we may know the effects of communication, we do not understand the means) and openness of the possibility that communication will not simply call to mind what we have already thought and said but achieve a new truth, something we have not already discovered. The question "why do precisely these objects which we behold make a world?" (150) is not dissimilar to the possible question "why do precisely these words which we behold make sense?" In some way they are equivalent and parallel questions, and equally as answerable and unanswerable. But to transgress the borders of the totality, either of the world or of language, which we had experienced is discovery or revelation. Thoreau's sentence regarding "a strain of music" itself tests these limits.

The possibility of transgressing our own limitations is the burden of the last sentences of *Walden* and its admonitions neither to be content with nor even to seek the influence of what has already been thought and said. It is perhaps, again, paradoxical for a writer to take the attitude toward language that it is inadequate to prepare us for truth to come. Yet it is a paradox persisting in theories of language, communication, education and learning, that the mind can discover new orientations and meanings outside those it inherits. Reiterating the metaphor that "we know not where we are," Thoreau's narrator then supposes that, just as by opening a hole in the ice we may find summer in winter, we also may discover other transpositions equally as illuminating. Inverting the order by which we are helpless to discover or invent anything new before a transcendent God, he writes:

Drive a nail home and clinch it so faithfully that you can wake up in the night and think of your work with satisfaction,—a work at which you would not be ashamed to invoke the Muse. So will help you God, and so only. Every nail driven should be as another rivet in the machine of the universe, you carrying on the work. (221)

As with beans, so with nails, it is not they literally nor you literally: Although they exist, they express something that escapes the "residual statement" of referring to them. Retelling a story (alluded to by Hawthorne and Melville and in circulation at the time) of a bug that hatched from the dry wood of "an old table of apple-tree wood," he asks: "Who does not feel his faith in a resurrection and immortality strengthened by hearing of this?" (222). Invoking these traditional terms of Christian theology and eschatology is itself an act of translation or transposition of the familiar to a new context. For Christians, traditionally, "immortality" is something promised after life; resurrection either an historical event in the life of Jesus or a future event at the end of history. Thoreau's narrator implicitly sets these meanings aside, for he has said both that "God himself culminates in the present moment" (65-66) and "Things do not change; we change" (219). (In terms later adopted by radical Christian theology, we would mistake the relations of the symbolic to the literal to suppose that the language of biblical expression equates historical with spiritual truth, rather than making one the vehicle for the other.) Resurrection becomes a metaphor for radical transformation of the self. Finally he concludes:

I do not say that John or Jonathan [names for the Englishmen and Americans, respectively] will realize all this; but such is the character of that morrow which mere lapse of time can never make to dawn. The light which puts out our eyes is darkness to us. Only that day dawns to which we are awake. There is more day to dawn. The sun is but a morning star. (223)

The relationships among these last sentences represent what rhetoricians call parataxis. Whether true or false, they seem to be related to each other without supplying those connective words and propositions that would tell us how they are related. That "the sun is but a morning star" is true metaphorically and literally, but something else seems implied by the statement; that "there is more day to dawn" seems likely in a literal sense, but what of it? "Only that day dawns to which we are awake" is true at least on assumptions that a radical empiricist would hold, and yet it seems to signify something more. Overall, the passage urges us to change our orientation, following the general pattern of the book, from desperation to expectation, to renew or refresh our will and motivation.

What is meant by "us" here and in the passage just quoted is worth exploring. To adopt a familiar distinction between audience invoked and audience implied, we note that the narrator begins by invoking a local audience of neighbors and townspeople (the "you who read these pages, who are said to live in New England" [2]), and of "poor students" (perhaps in multiple senses of the word "poor"). But here the "John or Jonathan" who are Thoreau's most likely immediate readers in his own time are referred to in the third person, as though to dissociate the reader from them or from their characters—or, more accurately, from their limitations. And so perhaps it is that Thoreau's narrator attempts to dissociate his receptive local audience from these stock characters, to cause such a reader to place himself beside himself (remaining within the gendered boundaries articulated here) and so to engage in thinking beside himself "in a sane sense." As literary critics point out, "irony" involves an implied double audience, one destined not to comprehend what is comprehended by a second and superior audience—an audience "beside itself" and therefore able to perceive the speaker's double meaning. So there also appears to be a projection of an audience here, implied but not invoked, of a future date or other location that will perform yet another transposition, that of this discourse into a time or place which is not "yarded" or within the same "bounds" as the more local and immediate one is. Such an implied transposition has the effect of generalizing the audience and the import of the book so that it is not, finally, only to or about or for or against this local and proscribed audience that the book is written, but (in one of Thoreau's favored allusions) to anyone who has ears to hear.

What Method or Manner of Philosophy is this?

It is characteristic of some kinds of religious discourse and of disciplines introducing neophytes to mysteries, and perhaps humanistic education in general, to suppose that one progresses from a misapprehension of the meaning of discourse and ritual toward a closer association with the truth without ever quite arriving at one's destination. Rather, one travels from approximation to closer approximation. One mistakes the symbolic for the literal, local for the universal, at different stages of the way, and must necessarily do so for the reasons that Thoreau's narrator states: The truth we aim at exceeds the boundaries of our language and our world. We both know, by approximation, and do not know, "where we are." The recovery of a sense of location and orientation is a continual process, described in *Walden*, not unlike the Christian process of turning toward God, which depends first upon the realization that one is dis-oriented:

> And not until we are completely lost, or turned round,—for a man must needs only to be turned around once with his eyes shut in this world to be lost,—do we appreciate the vastness and strangeness of Nature. Every man has to learn the points of the compass again as often as he awakes, whether from sleep or from any abstraction. Not till we are lost in other words, not till we have lost the world, do we begin to find ourselves, and realize where we are and the infinite extent of our relations. (115)

This yet again is another transposition of biblical precept—"whoever loses his life will preserve it" (Luke 17.33b)—based on the parable of Lot's wife who turned back to look at their lost estate (Genesis 19.26) rather than having faith in prophecy. It is also, at the same time, another original Thoreauvian parable of the need for reorientation. If our relations are indeed infinite, they are inexpressible. Any finite expression only stands in the way of the revelation of this extent and confuses us when we forget that it is finite.

The closest one comes in modern philosophy to a parallel to Thoreau's paradoxical but coherent views and practice is in portions of Wittgenstein's *Tractatus*, especially the latter part of 6, beginning perhaps with 6.373: "The world exists independently of my will." The parallel is striking between the two following passages—one on death and temporality and the other on method—and Thoreau's assertions:

> Death is not an event in life. Death is not lived through. If by eternity we mean not endless temporal duration but timelessness, then to live eternally is to live in the present. In the same way as our visual field is without boundary, our life is endless. (6.4311)

My sentences are illuminating in the following way: to

understand me you must recognize my sentences—once you have climbed out through them, over them, on them—as senseless. (You must, so to speak, throw away the ladder after you have climbed up on it.) You must climb out through my sentences; then you will see the world correctly. (6.54)

Put another way, the purpose of discourse is for conveyance rather than habitation; and the purpose of on-going discourse is not to build a world but to climb out of the misconstruction of residual statement into the light of sense, metaphorically speaking. This complicates the critique offered by Richard Poirier (cited in Chapter 1) inasmuch as that critique sees writers as attempting to create an "environment" that "has an existence only in style" (Poirier 17), unless we go on to say, as he does, that simultaneously their "activity of creation…denies finality to the results of that activity, its objects or formulations" (21). The purpose of Thoreau's discourse is not so much to set down rules of thought or to control thought as to incite thinking, as he urges the reader to do, and he leaves off the discourse (unless one insists that his prospective conclusion is a conclusion), as he left off living at Walden "for as good a reason as [he] went there" (215). That is all that is to be thought and said on that location. One can re-enter that environment of words, but the reiteration of the theme will not add to its structure or sense, change though our perceptions will on each (surprising) re-reading. One returns to it for the refreshment of being turned out again on its limbs, which leave us struggling with our own meanings and orientations in relation to those mapped here.

Discussion Questions

1. Choose a passage from *Walden* that has a particularly difficult or peculiar style for you: How does this passage exemplify or help us to understand Poirier's comment that the book creates an "environment" that "has an existence only in style"? Alternatively, consider any of Wittgenstein's propositions in the *Tractatus* as a parallel statement to some other(s) in *Walden*: To what degree do the two works illuminate or explicate each other?

2. Consider Thoreau's use of colloquial expressions such as "being beside oneself." Are there more literal equivalents to such expressions? What does Thoreau gain by the use of colloquialism? What other examples can you cite, and why are they significant? What do you think might be the difference

between speaking or thinking in colloquial (informal) language and speaking or thinking in abstract, philosophical (formal) language? Are the two possible kinds ever commingled in Thoreau's discourse?

3.   What function(s) does irony serve in Thoreau's writing? Is this consistent with serious or sincere thinking? Do other writers mentioned here—e.g., David Hume—display irony in their writing? How would you compare and contrast these writers on the basis of their use or avoidance of irony?

4.   Several "tropes" or "figures of speech" that Thoreau employs seem to parallel closely tropes and figures in the New Testament, in form or content. Examine one or more of these kinds of allusions and discuss what Thoreau gains in meaning by his close verbal parallels. How close or distant does he seem to be to a Christian worldview in his writing? How does the passage you have chosen illustrate this closeness or distance?

3

"Civil Disobedience" And Other Social Writings

One Honest Man

"Let your life be a counter-friction to stop the machine"—"Civil Disobedience" ("Resistance to Civil Government" 232)

Thoreau's essay called "Civil Disobedience" or "Resistance to Civil Government" (Thoreau's own title and that of its first publication) is generally printed following the text of *Walden* in trade and mass market editions of his work, although the essay was actually written earlier than the book and first published in 1848. Its central narrative portion concerns events that took place in 1846 when Thoreau was still living at Walden Pond and was arrested for refusing to pay the poll tax. The two works interrelate in some important ways, but they have distinctly different objectives and take different stylistic and rhetorical tacks to reach their aims. Succinctly put, "Civil Disobedience" aims to move the reader to action rather than to contemplation and reflection as does *Walden*. Contrasted with the complex linguistic patterns of *Walden*, the language of the essay is straightforwardly expository and its structure is demonstrably sermonic.

The year 1848 is significant as a year of European democratic revolutions and increasing sectional conflict in the United States over the issue of slavery (exacerbated by the Dred Scott Decision in ~~1847~~, 1857 holding that slaves were not citizens) despite a widespread sense of national purpose in the prosecution of the Mexican War—a war that Thoreau, Emerson, and others opposed as an imperialist attack on the sovereignty of another nation and an illicit extension of slavery. Thoreau delivered an early version of the essay as a lecture in January 1848, before the surrender of Mexico in February, and published it in April of that year. There is a tone of personal urgency in the essay. Active in the cause of assisting fugitive slaves on the "underground railroad" and opposed to standing armies, Thoreau makes the case against the current state of his government and for the radical primacy of the individual conscience against the State, which has no conscience except to the degree that those who comprise it influence its actions. ("It is not so important that many should be as good as you," he writes, "as that there be some absolute goodness somewhere; for that will leaven the whole lump," alluding to I Corinthians 5.6-8.) It is an extraordinarily radical document to have achieved so prominent a place among texts taught in high school curricula, though perhaps that inclusion itself is a domesticating factor.

In *Walden*, Thoreau had critiqued arrangements of contemporary life as "improved means to an unimproved end" (35), and here again the issue of the relationship of means to disputed ends is the crux of the argument. He argues, also, against government as a mere "tradition...each instant losing some of its integrity" (in phrases echoing his concern in *Walden* that meaning in language be "instantly translated"), lacking the "vitality and force of a single living man" (226), and against majority rule in those matters which do not concern mere expediency but right or justice. The pattern of the essay is similar to that of *Walden*, as well, moving from a sense of confinement within present circumstances to a vision of a "more perfect" future (245) which is not yet realized. From a clear and emphatic statement of the contradiction between apparent and actual circumstances, the rhetoric of the essay intensifies and personalizes the sense of contradiction to the point of insistence, even to the degree that the speaker mimics the visionary utterance of a Puritan conversion sermon, analogizing slavery and war to crucifixion: "I see this blood flowing now" (236). Precepts take precedence over parable (in contrast to the more iterative exposition of *Walden*) but these are continually related to parables and precepts of Jesus in the New

Testament with which Thoreau's audience would have been intimately familiar. The specificity of references to the Bible and the likeness of the essay in tenor and structure to a Christian sermon, however, do not limit its application only to those who would endorse Christian doctrine. Here, as elsewhere, we could say that Thoreau is engaged in a kind of transvaluation of Christian tropes and precepts, transposing them from one context of belief to another, from the Christian to the transcendental.

The content of transcendental belief is difficult and perhaps misleading to specify; but in speaking elsewhere of the response of Northern supporters of the abolitionist John Brown, Thoreau gives us a key:

> The North, I mean the *living* North, was suddenly all transcendental. It went behind the human law, it went behind the apparent failure, and recognized eternal justice and glory. ("Last Days," *Reform Papers* 147)

Not tropes and precepts but the percepts that give rise to them are the authorization of action, the meaning that escapes the dross of residual statement. In terms more common to political and moral philosophy, he holds that there must be a higher or anterior law—a law above or behind the law—that authorizes local and particular laws. (See Derrida's "Before the Law" for an analysis of the concept of law as requiring such an assumption.) Thus, while the influence of the essay can be felt in a specifically Christian social advocate such as Martin Luther King, Jr., it is by no means limited to a Christian audience. Despite its continual recourse to biblical allusion, it also influenced the decidedly non-Christian Mohandas Ghandi and provided a fundamental metaphor of the State as a machine for those who had no particular religious orientation but who opposed the Vietnam War.

At the same time, it would be a mistake to identify Thoreau's meaning with those whom he influenced who might be considered "liberal," "left wing," or "right wing" in the context of later politics. Thoreau poses the question of the virtue and authority of the State versus that of the individual in terms of a classical rather than a utilitarian liberalism. That is, his position is "liberal" (deriving from the Latin word "liberus," referring to "free men" [see "Last Days" 151]) in the sense of supporting a disposition toward the non-interference of government in the conduct of daily life, rather than toward the interference of government to achieve social justice through redistribution of goods. But it does not make the conservative turn toward affirmation of tradition and specifically the argument that a "strict construction" of the Constitution of 1789 allows slavery, and he does identify maintaining social good as a proper role of government ("A Plea" 130). He chastises Daniel Webster, for instance, who took a strict constructionist position, saying: "Webster never goes behind government, and so cannot speak with authority about it" ("Resistance" 243). As always with Thoreau, it is important to watch or to listen to the little words as well as the big ones: In becoming "transcendental," the North "went *behind* the human law" as Webster "never goes *behind* government."

The contradiction between the State and his conscience arises not because the State passively allows slavery to exist, but because the State actively enforces an artificial relation of dominance of one man over another, asserting the primacy of might rather than right. By doing so, he argues, the State contradicts itself. In terms of our contemporary journalistic and informal discourse of "leftwing," 'rightwing," and "middle of the road" politics, this position is nowhere on the scale. It is tempting even to say that it is not political at all but moral. (Thoreau himself consistently restricts his use of the term "political" to refer only to the merely expedient.) But perhaps it is most accurate to say that it renounces the most common political signposts as guides to action in favor of the radically inward direction of conscience.

The Argument

Thoreau refers to action under the direction of conscience as "action from principle"(233). In *Walden* he argues, somewhat obliquely, that it is necessary to find a "*point d'appui*, below freshet [flood] and frost and fire" (drawing his metaphor from stone masonry) to create a foundation for knowledge that is not a "freshet of shams and appearances" (*Walden* 66). Here he critiques those "statesmen and legislators....[who] speak of moving society, but have no resting place without it" (243). Whether the metaphor derives from building arts or from the Archimedes' notion of moving the world by the use of a fulcrum, the point is that a system or machine can only be designed and made to operate according to a principle that is not identical with its mere parts—something that transcends the relations of individual parts and their materiality. With respect to the State, the individual supplies the principle: There will never be a really free and

51

enlightened State, until that State comes to recognize the individual as a higher and independent power, from which all its own power and authority are derived, and treats him accordingly" ("Resistance" 245). This puts a highly individualistic twist on the founding tenets of the American republic articulated in the Declaration of Independence, that governments "deriv[e] their just powers from the consent of the governed." If Thoreau has in mind such a text as this, he silently assumes rather than directly argues that "the governed" or "the people" resolve into individuals or rather "the individual." Once again, we seem to encounter embedded in his discourse the theory of the "one man" who is divided according to functions and who misperceives himself as many men. As he elsewhere says: "It is for want of a man that there are so many men" ("Life Without Principle," *Reform Papers* 171). However that ontological or speculative problem may be resolved, he insists that:

> Action from principle,—the perception and performance of right,—changes things and relations; it is essentially revolutionary, and does not consist with anything which was. It not only divides states and churches, it divides families; aye, it divides the individual, separating the diabolical in him from the divine. ("Resistance" 233)

The passage echoes the reported words of Jesus that would soon become the touchstone for a famous speech by Lincoln and a fundamental metaphor for the division of the Republic: "Do you suppose that I came to bring peace on earth? I tell you, not at all, but rather division. From now on five in a house will be divided: three against two and two against three…"(Luke 12.51-52).

The idea that "[principle] divides the individual" returns us to the matter of being beside oneself, though it is not clear that there is symmetry between the duality of spectator and actor and that of "diabolical" and "divine." Nor is there any immediate non-personal or trans-personal standard by which to judge perceptions and intentional acts as divine or diabolical, since all manifest signs and sources of truth are but partial, and truth itself remains transcendent:

> They who know no purer sources of truth, who have traced its stream up no higher, stand, and wisely stand, by the Bible and the Constitution, and drink at it there with reverence and humility; but they who behold where it comes trickling into this lake or that

pool, gird up their loins once more, and continue their pilgrimage toward its fountainhead. ("Resistance" 244)

The Bible and the Constitution are treated as particular and local manifestations of truth, as in *Walden* historically defined languages are treated as mere dialects, affirmed by tradition and useful as they are limited: What is transcendent *is* transcendent. Like other tropes for futurity and truth, this one entails a paradox that Thoreau would know from exploration. As one proceeds to find the source or fountainhead of a river one never comes to a single point that one can call its source, for rivers are as dispersed in their origins as in their destinations. The pilgrimage is either unending or ends with the perception that all things return to a source that is transcendent and indefinable.

So summarized, the essay would seem to be based in a vicious circularity, for it appears that the individual is a part rather than the whole of the State, existing as a subject rather than him- or herself as the embodiment of transcendent principle. The statement that "a single man can bend it [the American government] to his will" seems to return us to the criterion of might rather than right. What Thoreau assumes and only implies, however, is that the sense and perception of right and wrong only exists in individuals, and his argument is first and foremost an epistemological one, that "right" is ultimately more persuasive because it is more consistent with self-regard than "might":

> Can there not be a government in which majorities do not decide right and wrong, but conscience?—in which majorities decide only those questions to which the rule of expediency is applicable? Must every citizen ever for a moment, or in the least degree, resign his conscience to the legislator? Why has every man a conscience, then? I think that we should be men first, and subjects afterward. (227)

In *Walden*, Thoreau's narrator comments that "we commonly do not remember that it is always the first person that is speaking" in order to critique the habitual (and perhaps, for Thoreau, the habitually American) tendency to cite the popular opinion by invoking the third person, "they say," thereby disowning one's own person-hood. Only the first person, the individual, can originate discourse with reference to a philosophically conceived "subject," and thus only the individual has access (however mediated) to the thought of categories such as "right" and "wrong," or "true" and "false." Indeed, "Nature puts no question and answers none which we mortals ask" (*Walden* 188). Only the "human entity" can "suppose a case" and take action under the direction of a choice between alternatives. (It is, after all, the legal basis for the judgment of the competency of persons to be able to distinguish between right and wrong.) "The only obligation," he writes in "Civil Disobedience," "which I have a right to assume, is to do at any time what I think is right"'(227). And "what I think is right" is defined not by reference to expediency but to the idea of justice. So it is in the example that Thoreau uses to illustrate the difference between cases in which expediency applies and cases in which it does not: "If I have unjustly wrested a plank from a drowning man, I must restore it to him though I drown myself" (229). Justice is not equivalent, then, to mere individual whim or assertion of the will. The sense of "right" may persuade us, in some cases must persuade us, to act against self-interest. Insofar as Thoreau coordinates his assertion of the primacy of principle to any prior text or doctrine, it is again by allusion to the New Testament, when he paraphrases (immediately after the sentence just quoted) Jesus' words as reported by Luke "But he that would save his life, in such a case, shall lose it" (229; cf. Luke 9.24). As in a sermon, the speaker's concern is not so much to prove the truth of such precepts as to make them operative and apply them, which he does immediately following: "This people must cease to hold slaves, and to make war on Mexico, though it cost them their existence as a people" (230). The obligation of the individual to do right is the obligation of the aggregate of individuals: "It is truly enough said [in standard legal theory], that a corporation has no conscience; but a corporation of conscientious men is a corporation *with* a conscience" (227). Individuals are not relieved of obligations belonging to them and to them alone by participating in an aggregate.

To Murder or to Die: The Dilemma of Slavery

The issue of slavery is central to the force of Thoreau's argument not only because it is topically important but because it presents a case of the unmitigated assertion of might over right and against the defining characteristic of human entities, freedom or the ability to choose. Thoreau takes his audience to agree that slavery is wrong in this way and to differ from him mainly by endorsing intervening arguments or rationalizations or mere talk which inhibit "action from principle." Again, this makes the essay like a sermon in which the preacher establishes the principle from which the rhetorical appeal to action (whether of "the heart," "mind," or "body") follows and then argues against the audience's resistance to accepting the immediate application of the principle: "Unjust laws exist: shall we be content to obey them, or shall we endeavor to amend them, and obey them until we have succeeded, or shall we transgress them at once?" (233).

By implication, to acquiesce to unjust laws when confronted with them is not merely to endorse but to prosecute them. One does not have to go out of one's way to reform laws or government, because one does have the right, like others, to be left alone. But not to oppose injustice when one meets it "face to face" (234), not as mere writing but as the action of men, is to enter into or acquiesce in a "copartnership" with injustice. Thus, in what appears to be a leap of logic or *non sequitur*, "Under a government which imprisons any unjustly, the true place for a just man is also in prison" (235). But the underlying logic of this transition is that in prison just men are "locked out of the [unjust] State by her own act, as they have already put themselves out by their principles," for the State "places those who are not *with* her...*against* her" (235). The prison is symbolic of this out-placing and opposition to the State; the underlying meaning resides in opposition.

Thoreau holds that purposeful opposition to slavery, based on principle, would defeat slavery:

> [I]f one thousand, if one hundred, if ten men whom I could name,—if ten honest men only,—aye if one HONEST man, in this State of Massachusetts, ceasing to hold slaves, were actually to withdraw from this copartnership, and be locked up in the county jail therefor, it would be the abolition of slavery in America. (234)

The form of opposition he suggests is, however, passive. Subsequent applications of his message have endorsed what is called a "passive resistance" to injustice on the theory that repeated acts of out-placing oneself, of ceasing to cooperate in injustice, by dramatic but symbolic action will either force others to a recognition of injustice (by, for instance, confronting the spectacle of the just man in prison) or simply wear away the will of agents of the State to do wrong in the guise of enforcing the law. But it is not clear that Thoreau is as tactically inclined here as subsequent practitioners of civil disobedience would be (and he does not anticipate the reserves of repressive tolerance on the part of the State). In concluding this essay, he does not emphasize practical consequences, but performs a double action of recalling his audience to the force of the revelation which he has just said is only partial and projecting a vision of a future state:

> For eighteen hundred years, though perchance I have no right to say it, the New Testament has been written; yet where is the legislator who has wisdom and practical talent enough to avail himself of the light which it sheds on the science of legislation? ....I please myself with imagining a State which at last can afford to be just to all men, and to treat the individual with respect as a neighbor; which even would not think it inconsistent with its own repose, if a few were to live aloof from it, nor embraced by it, who fulfilled all the duties as neighbors and fellow-men. A State which bore this kind of fruit, and suffered it to drop off as fast as it ripened, would prepare the way for a still more perfect State, which I have also imagined, but not yet anywhere seen. (244-245)

The memorable precepts of the New Testament—"do unto others...," "render unto Caesar...," and many others—are imagined in his peroration as articulations of a proto-science of legislation that might be crafted and even perfected in the progress of humankind (briefly outlined from absolute to limited monarchy and thence to democracy [245]). On one hand, the current state of government, as critiqued here, does not, then, even live up to this heritage of the speaker and the audience. On the other, it does not live up to an imagined future state, but exists betwixt and between, in a kind of netherworld. The challenge is "to take a step further toward recognizing and organizing the rights of man" by recognizing "the individual as a higher and independent power" (245), but the politics of such a recognition are not laid out except in terms of a passive tolerance that would allow "a few to live aloof from" the State. Unlike projectors of utopian communities, Thoreau does not plan the social organization he envisions (in fact he often expresses that he would have been content with what he *thought* was the society to which he belonged), being at once both more transcendental and more realistic than they would be.

It is perhaps an index of Thoreau's transcendental innocence in the field of politics (not entirely unlike Emerson's initial innocence in the field of epistemology) that he does not really ask in this early example of his social writing why the State exists beyond its function as a facilitator of trade. Yet it does exist, and he sees it as an affront to the self-respect of its members that in existing it enforces injustice rather than justice. But he also believes that a "more perfect State" could exist. He is not an anarchist in an absolute sense, and his collected social writings are aptly called *Reform Papers*. As his narrator in *Walden* portrays himself waking on a winter morning to imagine transpositions of the winter scene into summer, and stitching the tattered edge of community into a whole garment, so Thoreau seems in his social writings to attempt to imagine that things can be better than they are. He is perhaps among the sincerest believers that the State ought to be just.

Others, of the school of expediency, have believed otherwise. If Thoreau seems surprised that the State requires that a person surrender his or her person-hood, other philosophers have seen the transactions of the individual with the State as a kind of sleight of hand in which one surrenders person-hood for the purpose of the preservation of physical life, banding with others against yet others who would murder or rob or enslave oneself, for self-protection. Such is the view, for instance, of Hobbes in *Leviathan*. For Hobbes, without the protection of the State, one is subject to being murdered by anyone stronger that oneself, and the State has its origin in the desire for the protection of life and liberty—in mutual fear of destruction. Thus the State is an expediency that temporally mediates a person's dilemma in the state of nature—to murder or to die—and that assumes the transcendent position of control over life and death as a "Mortal God" (Hobbes 114). In a regime of representative government, subjects "reduce all their wills, by a plurality of voices, unto one will." In this State, the subject may not refuse the order to murder or to be killed if such refusal "frustrates the end for which the sovereignty was ordained," but may do so if such refusal does not contradict the end for which government is instituted (145).

But such a theory does not resolve the dilemma of slavery, since slavery incorporates within the State the absolute dominion of one person over another, so that the master is life and the slave is death, reduced to a thing, a non-person, or an extension of the master's consciousness and freedom. (See Hegel, *The Phenomenology of Mind*, B. IV. B. 3; Frederick Douglass, *Narrative*, especially Chapter X; and Von Frank 141-142). The struggle between master and slave is nothing less than a life or death struggle at the level of consciousness and social being, and the dilemma for anyone implicated in the regime of slavery (master, slave, spectator) is the same: to murder or to die. Only the abolition of the contradiction, man and slave in one body, can resolve the dilemma.

The Case of Anthony Burns: Self and Other

Such views of slavery and freedom are equally grounded in fable—that is, narrative that explains action—to any views Thoreau might have, attempting to find an explanation of where we find ourselves in a reasonable story of origin. Fables provide explanatory paradigms for existing conditions between human beings, abstracting from experience and giving momentary concretion to fugitive and dispersed relations. Such stories are attuned to the limitations of the law: that "the law will never make men free" ("Slavery in Massachusetts," *Reform Papers* 98), but only provides subjects with temporal liberty in the sense of the possibility of a range of action without interference from others, which is always conditional, so that "it is men who have got to make the law free." In the case of slavery, only the repeal of laws that enact slavery can result in freedom; the law itself is bondage. It happens that many slaves were relatively at liberty, such as Anthony Burns, *within bounds*, but not free when they skipped those bounds from a Slave State, like Virginia, to a supposedly Free State, like Massachusetts. There Burns was arrested and imprisoned in 1854 awaiting a trial to decide whether he should be remanded to his putative "owner" in Virginia. The case is the occasion of Thoreau's writing "Slavery in Massachusetts," which transforms his claims regarding actions occasioned by his personal encounter with the State, in "Civil Disobedience," to claims based on the occasion of the public trial regarding another "human entity."

Prior to his alleged "escape" from Stafford County, Virginia, Burns had been one of a class of slaves "hired out" for work at wages by their masters, who were therefore considerably more at liberty than plantation or work gang slaves more commonly associated with the plantation South. (Frederick Douglass belonged for some part of his slave life to this class.) Having escaped from Virginia to Boston, Burns was arrested on a warrant for his return in late May 1854. The case aroused the abolitionist community first to legal and symbolic and then to direct action. Thoreau's "Slavery in Massachusetts" has its immediate origin in notes for a lecture at an anti-slavery rally at Framingham, Massachusetts, on July 4, 1854, in which Thoreau took only a small part, and it focuses on Burns's case (as did other speeches) as the most prominent current example of the injustice of the State, not in Virginia or at the Federal level, but in Massachusetts:

"Again it happens [as in the case of Thomas Sims in 1851] that the Boston Court House is full of armed men, holding prisoner and trying a MAN, to find out if he is not really a SLAVE"(92). The situation amplifies Thoreau's continual contention (also part of his argument in "Civil Disobedience") that the issue of slavery is not a matter of what happens to others somewhere else but a local and immediate concern to people in Massachusetts.

The ironies of the Burns case were not lost on any of the abolitionist commentators on it. (See Von Frank, *The Trials of Anthony Burns.*) Certainly Thoreau responded to and exploited those ironies. A difference between this and other writings, however, is the marked lack of irony in his voice (which engages rather in blunt sarcasm) and the dominance of ascription of irony to the situation. If in other cases, Thoreau is willing to say that a conflict of suppositions amounts to a necessary doubleness of consciousness, there can be no mediation of the contradiction embedded in Burns's case: One cannot be both a slave and a man. Burns is a man. Therefore, Burns is not a slave and any court that judges him such is an affront to God and reason. Thoreau has advanced in taking personally the affront to justice, abdicating the distance he had placed between himself as spectator and other enactors of a social spectacle in works such as *Walden* and "Civil Disobedience." Consequently, he imagines himself not in a netherworld of ambiguity, betwixt and between truth and falsehood, but in a world in which intuitive distinctions between right and wrong, the dictates of conscience, are wholly and perversely reversed:

> I have lived for the last month,—and I think that every man in Massachusetts capable of the sentiment of patriotism must have had a similar experience,—with the sense of having suffered a vast and indefinite loss. I did not know at first what ailed me. At last it occurred to me that what I had lost was a country. I had never respected the Government near to which I had lived, but I had foolishly thought that I might live here, minding my private affairs, and forget it. For my part, my oldest and worthiest pursuits have lost I cannot say how much of their attraction, and I feel that my investment in life is worth many per cent[.] less since Massachusetts last deliberately sent back an innocent man, Anthony Burns, to slavery. I dwelt before, perhaps, in the illusion that my life passed somewhere only *between* heaven and hell, but

now I cannot persuade myself that I do not dwell *wholly within* hell....I feel that, to some extent, the State has fatally interfered with my lawful business. It has not only interrupted me in my passage through Court street on errands of trade, but it has interrupted every man on his onward and upward path, on which he had trusted soon to leave Court street far behind. What right had it to remind me of Court street? I have found that hollow which even I had relied on to be solid. (106-107)

In saying "which even I had relied on," of course, Thoreau acknowledges that he was among those least likely to think of institutions as solid and substantial. But having been once arrested himself, and having let it pass with comment as an errancy of government, he now takes the arrest of another person as an even stronger affront. The strength of Thoreau's identification with Burns is remarkable—for it was Burns who was arrested in Court Street—and perhaps stronger than anyone would deduce from the mere application of abstract principle. Framing the situation as he does through this identification, Thoreau reduces the merely probable consideration (when government is considered as an expedient to liberty) of "If government does this to him, what might it do to me, or what would it do to me, under similar circumstances?" to the more direct proposition "As the government has done to him, so it has done to me." He says that he can do without a Governor because "If he is not the least use to prevent my being kidnapped, pray of what important use is he likely to be to me?" (92). Thoreau places no distance or difference of class or circumstance between himself and the supposed slave, enacting in his thought the basis of the fable of the "one man" who exists despite apparent differences.

It is perhaps difficult in a later day to appreciate the specific weight of the word "patriotism" in Thoreau's discourse, and the importance of allegiance to particular States of the Union. Patriotism was a more local and familial feeling in the context of pre-Civil War America than it is in a modern mass nation-state—and especially so in Concord. The feeling was one of actual personal gratitude to those "patriots" who had secured such rights for themselves as *habeas corpus*, the right to be secure in one's person, to associate freely, and the like. It entailed, as well, a sense of personal responsibility to ensure that those rights were maintained not only against foreign intervention but against domestic encroachment. To allow the suspension of *habeas corpus* in any circumstance would be unpatriotic. For the government to suspend it in the normal conduct of events would be a contradiction in terms, an affront to one's own patriotism. By technicalities of law, however, amounting to gross contradictions in the law itself, *habeas corpus* did not apply to Anthony Burns, since the law did not regard him as a person but as an article of property. But for abolitionists and for Thoreau it ought to apply, since Burns was evidently a man, and one could not be both a man and a slave. The failure of a court and court officer at once to recognize Burns's humanity and the incoherence of law was appalling, leading Thoreau to egregious metaphor:

> Much has been said about American slavery, but I think that we do not even yet realize what slavery is. If I were seriously to propose to Congress to make mankind into sausages, I have no doubt that most of the members would smile at my proposition, and if any one believe me in earnest, they would think that I proposed something much worse than I had ever done. But if any of them tell me that to make a man into a sausage would be much worse,—would be any worse, than to make him into a slave,— than it was to enact the Fugitive Slave Law, I will accuse him of foolishness, of intellectual incapacity, of making a distinction without a difference. (96-97)

The sausage metaphor uncannily anticipates what could almost be thought literally under subsequent racist regimes, such as Nazism. Its effectiveness either for the converted who may have heard the speech or read it or for those who continued to support slavery or the provisions of the Fugitive Slave law is however questionable. One commentator of the time described the speech as "racy," and there is a great deal in it, including this passage, that could be considered so. But it does seem to take away from the central and simpler thought to deprive any human being of fundamental rights is to deprive everyone, to deprive me, of such rights.

It would have been all the more simple for his contemporary hearers given their memory of a revolution their grandfathers had fought and a living tradition of patriotism—more simple, that is, but for the intervening fact of a racism which Thoreau appears to have seen clearly through. His conclusion is, again, in parts biblically prophetic:

I am surprised to see men going about their business as if nothing has happened....Fool! does he not know that his seed-corn is worth less this year—that all beneficent harvests fail as you approach the empire of hell....It is not an era of repose. We have used up all our inherited freedom. If we would save our lives, we must fight for them. (107-108)

In other parts it is ominously treasonous, as when he says: "My thoughts are murder to the State, and involuntarily go plotting against her" (108). He attempts, as in other previous works, to end with a hopeful note, claiming that "slavery and servility...have no real life" and merely wait to be buried (109). But these thoughts are not tied either to the prospective dawning of a symbolic new day nor to any particular action, and so fail rhetorically and thematically. Yet the idea of "murder" and "plotting" are hauntingly predictive.

The Case of John Brown

The idea that one man should act upon the prompting of his conscience to seek justice is tested severely in the case of John Brown. Brown was a committed abolitionist whose commitments led him to violent action in the struggle over the determination of Kansas as a "slave" or "free" State (he killed five purported supporters of slavery in actions related to what amounted to a civil war in the territory) and in an attack on a Federal Arsenal at Harpers Ferry, Virginia (now West Virginia), in 1859. Brown settled the dilemma of "to murder or to die" personally by choosing "to murder" in the cause of justice. Eventually, he himself was hanged after a trial for the assault at Harpers Ferry and became a martyr for abolitionists. Indirectly, he chose "to die" as well as "to murder," enabling a hagiography that would compare him to Christ, and in the combination of his choices he clearly denounced any compromise, on any terms, with the existence of slavery.

Thoreau had met Brown through his friend and fellow abolitionist Franklin Sanborn in early 1857. Subsequently, he was to be among Brown's foremost defenders in three addresses memorializing his cause: "A Plea for Captain John Brown," "Martyrdom of John Brown," and "The Last Days of John Brown" (*Reform Papers* 111-53). Brown's actions clearly resulted from his commitment to a principle rather than self-interest, and they were not undertaken in self-defense or any other traditionally mediating circumstance of violence. He transgressed a line that others toed between the symbolic and the real. If his actions did not have the consequence of freeing slaves immediately, they contributed to the calling of the question between pro- and anti-slavery factions in the years immediately preceding the Civil War. As Melville depicted him, perhaps borrowing from Thoreau ("Last Days" 145, 152), he was "the meteor of the war" and "weird," meaning truthful and prophetic ("The Portent," not published until 1865). For Thoreau and some others, he was a prophet comparable to Christ.

Among the triptych of essays devoted to Brown, "Martyrdom" is actually a brief pastiche of poems and translations read at a memorial service. "A Plea" and "Last Days" are the more substantial. Each ends with an important and characteristic turn for Thoreau, and each rests on the articulation of principles found in "Civil Disobedience." What is different is the fact of Brown himself having forced the issue of reckoning with the dilemma of living as a free man in an un-free country. For Thoreau, the characteristic ills of society result largely from the deferment of reckoning, and Brown becomes the paradigmatic man of judgment and action from principle—to the degree that the comparisons he enlists in depicting Brown seem astounding and, indeed, seem to be meant to astound.

In "A Plea," Thoreau compares Brown in rather quick succession to "the best of those who stood at Concord Bridge" (at the onset of the American Revolution), Ethan Allen, Cromwell and the Puritans, and Christ. In outlining Brown's lineage, Thoreau is careful to note that "he did not go the college called Harvard" and "was not fed on the pap that is there furnished," but went "to the great university of the West" (113), thus establishing the note of action against mere words: "He would have left a Greek accent slanting the wrong way, and righted up a falling man" (113). The opposition of word to deed sets up the main contrast of the essay—he does what the best of others in the contemporary scene only profess or discuss—without losing control of the subject that Brown was "a man of rare common sense and directness of speech, as of action; a transcendentalist above all, a man of ideas and principles" (115). The opposition allows Thoreau both to criticize his contemporaries and to answer the charge that Brown had run amok rather than acted from principle.

Essentially, the question of sanity devolves, for those who raise it in Brown's case, to the question of probity and self-interest as opposed to acting on one's sense of what is right. Thoreau's defense that a person may in fact know what is right, against all his neighbors, appeals to self-consistency and the sense of being at one within

63

oneself. The figure of being beside oneself appears again as an accusation that those who think that Brown is insane know not whom (or where) they are, while he is justly aware of himself:

> Any man knows when he is justified, and all the wits in the world cannot enlighten him on that point. The murderer always knows that he is justly punished; but when a government takes the life of a man without the consent of his conscience, it is an audacious government, and is taking a step toward its own dissolution. Is it not possible that as individual may be right and a government may be wrong? (136)

In "Last Days," he writes, "[Brown] best understood his position....Comparatively, all other men...were beside themselves" (145); that is—not sane. Those who accuse Brown of insanity do so because they lack courage, "for they know that they could never act as he does, as long as they are themselves" (121); which is to say that they are hypocrites who are divided against themselves and their own consciences:

> What right have you to enter into a compact with yourself that you will do thus or so, against the light within you? Is it for you to make up your mind—to form any resolution whatever—and not accept the convictions that are forced upon you, and which ever pass your understanding? (137)

The chief reason for the charge of insanity, that Brown would necessarily fail to achieve his immediate objectives, is held by Thoreau as moot: "I do not wish to kill or be killed, but I can foresee circumstances in which both of these things would be by me unavoidable" (133). In any case it raises the question, again, of whether one has actually lived:

> This event advertises me that there is such a fact as death—the possibility of a man's dying. It seems as if no man ever died in America before, for in order to die you must first have lived....The best of them ran fairly down like a clock. Franklin—Washington—they were left of without dying; they were merely missing one day (134).

Rhetorically (perhaps even logically), the fact of death presupposes life and enables the series of paradoxical tropes by which Thoreau analogizes Brown to Christ. He is not simply the "one honest man" Thoreau calls for in "Civil Disobedience," but a transcendent teacher: "These men [Brown and company], in teaching us how to die, have at the same time taught us how to live" (134).

Life as a bounded and finite sequence of actions—comedy or tragedy—makes no sense without a concept of death, and death makes sense only as that which liberates life into the infinity of its relations. The many analogies Thoreau draws between Brown and Christ amplify the sense that death bespeaks, in a very Puritan sense, the quality of life: "I plead not for his life, but for his character—his immortal life," indeed he says "I *almost fear* that I may yet hear of his deliverance, doubting if a prolonged life, if *any* life, can do as much good as his death" (137). Only the end of a story can prove its instruction; a story that does not end has no moral or significance.

Both "A Plea" and "Last Days" end with a characteristic Thoreauvian glance at futurity as the fulfillment of the significance of this particular story, a moment of realization that re-circulates the general through the particular and back to the general again:

> I foresee the time when the painter will paint that scene, no longer going to Rome for a subject; the poet will sing it; the historian will record it; and, with the Landing of the Pilgrims and the Declaration of Independence, it will be the ornament of some future national gallery, when at least the present form of Slavery shall be no more here. We shall then be at liberty to weep for Captain John Brown. Then, and not till then, will we take our revenge. ("A Plea" 138)

> On the day of his translation, I heard, to be sure, that he was *hung*, but I did not know what that meant; I felt no sorrow on that account; but not for a day or two did I even *hear* that he was *dead*, and not after any number of days shall I believe it. Of all the men who were said to be my contemporaries, it seemed to me that John Brown was the only one who *had not died*. I never hear of any man named Brown now,—and I hear of them pretty often,—I never hear of any particularly brave and earnest man, but my first thought is of John Brown, and what relation he may be to him. I meet him at every turn. He is more alive than he ever was. He is not confined to North Elba nor to Kansas. He is no longer working in secret. He works in public, and in the clearest

65

light that shines on this land. ("Last Days" 152-53)

This apotheosis of Brown in effect translates him from physical being to transcendent principle in a manner reserved, typically, for the greatest heroes.

Futurity, Looking Backward

The ethical ideal of dying for a cause is easier for us to conceive than the ethical justification of killing for a cause, not least because two of the paradigmatic individuals Karl Jaspers cites at the beginning of four historical traditions are known for their modes of dying. In dying for a cause, we assume, knowledge and will come together in a significant act. In killing or murder, as in the legal killing undertaken by the State in capital cases, knowledge is often uncertain and will unknown, despite Thoreau's idealization of the murderer who knows he is justly punished. John Brown as the paradigmatic individual of Thoreau's critique remains an ambiguous figure, and he has not been endorsed in the sort of futurity Thoreau projected. Not that some painters (such as Jacob Lawrence) and poets (such as Melville) have not treated the subject; but Brown's hanging and the bloody ground of Kansas have not entered into the pantheon of images of significant American events as Thoreau imagined. The transposition of the Christian mystery of life, death, and resurrection onto Brown's life and death claims for him a transcendent reality that would partially be fulfilled in the sense of mission of abolitionists and Union soldiers singing "John Brown's Body" and, later, "The Battle Hymn of the Republic" as they marched to the war Brown did much to precipitate. But these would not become dominant motifs for American culture. His violence would be suppressed in a tradition that imagined death and sacrifice as acts of liberation, but not murder. He remains an outsider hero, like the labor organizer Joe Hill in the ballad that memorializes him ("Said Joe, 'I never died'"). His meaning does not exceed the meaning of Christ in the Christian tradition. Brown may be the "one honest man" Thoreau calls for in "Civil Disobedience," but he is only the similitude of his putative precursor: "For as by one man's disobedience many were made sinners, so also by one Man's obedience many will be made righteous" (Romans 5.19). In Thoreau's world, there is no hierarchy in which one agent can intercede for others, or needs to, in this spiritual way. Brown's attempted intercession was social and we cannot pretend it to be more than that,

66

which would be enough but for the metaphorical frame Thoreau has chosen. Such is the necessary consequence of humanizing the Christian tradition. Each person is responsible for the dictates of his or her conscience. In the aftermath of Brown's ordeal, Thoreau reflected: "It is remarkable, but on the whole it is well, that it did not prove the occasion for a new sect of *Brownites* being formed in our midst" ("Last Days" 146). And we could agree.

Overall, Thoreau's social reform writings provide a sort of American prophecy pointing up the difference between present circumstances and originary ideals, recalling people to the transcendent principles "behind" law and custom and forcing readers to reflect on the habits of deferment and excuse that keep them from action. They do so perhaps more consistently than any other politically motivated speech in our history and literature. On the whole that too is well for them if not for our history.

Discussion Questions

1. Read the portions of Hobbes' *Leviathan* from which the quotations above are taken. Does Thoreau principally argue against or from Hobbes' arguments? How do the two thinkers differ/agree in their assumptions about political or social life?
2. Consider the various ways in which Thoreau employs the phrase "beside oneself" and its variations. Is he consistent in his meaning(s)? How so?
3. Cite an example of Thoreau's transposition of one of the sayings of Jesus from the biblical context to his own and describe how this changes the meaning of the saying or revises a common understanding of the context to which it is applied.

4

Thoreau as Naturalist

Poetry into Science

"We must look for a long time before we can see."–"Natural History of Massachusetts" (*Natural History Writings* 29)

The name "Thoreau" is nearly synonymous for many people with the word "nature," although they assume perhaps too easily that a book such as *Walden* is primarily about something we would commonly call nature—meaning water, trees, plants, soils, and undomesticated animals. As we have seen it is something more and other than that, even while those objects are part of what compose its referential world. Thoreau is a writer about nature, "improved" or cultivated and "unimproved" and wild, primarily in relation to the human presence in it, as a number of recent writers have made us aware (Donahue; Foster; Mitchell). In what sense and how he writes about nature in his "natural history" essays and his journals is as unique and individual as the manner in which he writes about other topics such consciousness or social reform. At the same time, his style and approach in writing about nature is specifiable within a spectrum of approaches from the conventionally "poetic" to the "scientific," although nearly anyone's first impulse would be to identify him more strongly with the poetic. Indeed, there are times when Thoreau appears to disparage the scientific in favor of the poetic: "That is a scientific account of the fact," he writes of the chemical explanation of why leaves change color in the fall, "—only a reassertion of the fact" ("Autumnal Tints," *Natural History Essays* 138); and, "How differently the poet and the naturalist look at objects!" (174).

Not surprisingly for Thoreau, however, a stance that begins in disparagement and negation generally finds its way to the affirmation of a synthesis (albeit with the experiential and poetic dominating) between opposed terms. Thus, in his earliest published writing on natural history, he begins his closing paragraph in a mood of dejection: "These volumes deal much in measurements and minute descriptions, not interesting to the general reader, with only here and there a colored sentence to allure him, like those plants growing in dark forests, which bear only leaves without blossoms" ("Natural History of Massachusetts" *Natural History Essays* 28). He goes on, however, to encourage the reader: "Let us not underrate the value of a fact; it will one day flower into a truth" (28). And then, noting how much of the natural history of "any animal" or "man himself" remains to be written, he as much as writes a job description for the "true" (and future) "man of science," balancing past and future as in the closing of so many works:

> Slow are the beginnings of philosophy. He has something demoniacal in him, who can discern a law or couple two facts. We can imagine a time when 'Water runs down hill' may have been taught in schools. The true man of science will know better by his finer organization; he will smell, taste, see, hear, feel, better than other men. His will be a deeper and finer experience. We do not learn by inference and deduction, but by direct intercourse and sympathy. It is with science as with ethics, —we cannot know the truth by contrivance and method; the Baconian is as false as any other, and with all the helps of machinery and the arts, the most scientific will still be the healthiest and friendliest man, and possess a more perfect Indian wisdom. ("Natural History of Massachusetts" 29)

Historians of science can refer us here, in tracing the idea of "coupl[ing] two facts" to the theory of "consilience" (a word resurrected recently by Edward O. Wilson) in which "Facts are not only brought together, but seen in a new point of view....[And] a new mental Element is superinduced...," creating a "new conception," resulting from "a principle of connexion and unity, supplied by the mind" (Whewell 153, 139, 163; quoted in Walls 11). If Thoreau had not grasped this idea from William Whewell, then it was available to him even more directly in Wordsworth's famous formulation:

> Imagination... has no reference to images that are merely a faithful copy, existing in the mind, of absent external objects; but is a word of higher import, denoting the operations of the mind upon those objects, and processes of creation or of fixed composition, governed by certain fixed laws....[C]onferring additional properties upon an object, or abstracting from it some of those which it actually possesses...thus enabling it to react upon the mind which hath performed the process, like a new existence. (Preface to *Poems* [1815] xx-xxi, xxv)

Regardless of where Thoreau got his phrasing and conception from, the effect of his peroration in "The Natural History of Massachusetts" is to steal back the idea of the "man of science" for the humanistic and integrative conception of science as opposed to a mechanistic and operationalist view. The parallel between Whewell and Wordsworth suggests a deeper parallel that it is possible to discern in modes of perception that lead to discovery through observation and reflection. (It is important to note that, in contrast to either Whewell or Wordsworth, Thoreau does not foreclose on the question of the origin of ideas, referring some to the external sensations or the memory of sensations and others to the mind alone. Even in referring to life as "a kind of fiction, a work of the imagination only" in *Walden* [91], he refers to the point of view of the aspect of the self he calls "the spectator." As we will see, Thoreau does not make the traditional, categorical division of man and nature.) The history of science no doubt bypassed this rhetorical moment of attempted reconciliation between poetry and science—among other reasons because of the burgeoning scientific activity spurred by the invention of devices for measurement and computation and the expanding fields they opened for inquiry. But, wisely, Thoreau had not denied the importance of "measurements and minute descriptions," only their lack of interest to the "general reader." Paradoxically, it was that lack of interest that most probably contributed to a lack of exploration of Thoreau's more strictly scientific writings after his death—some of which are only being winnowed out from his manuscripts several lifetimes later.

Finally, on the matter of the "man of science," it is not surprising to find that Thoreau also notes the effect of the division of labor and the professionalizing of what was to become not the "man of science" but the "scientist" (a word that did not gain general use until the mid-nineteenth century). Throughout his natural history writings, Thoreau comments on the harm that the division of labor does to our knowledge, so that knowledge of nature is a kind of triumph over abstraction and selection that results not from the play of the imagination but from a limitation of focus:

> A man sees only what concerns him. A botanist absorbed in the study of grasses does not distinguish the grandest pasture oaks. He, as it were, tramples down oaks unwittingly in his walk, or at most only sees their shadows. (*Natural History Essays* 174)

He continues the illustration through several different sorts of persons and concerns, and he makes a similar point in the posthumously published essay "Huckleberries." Here he compares the view of the "professional huckleberry picker," landowner, cook, and ends with the botanist:

> While Professor D. –for whom the pudding is intended, sits in his library reading a book—a work that deals with the *Vaccinieae* of course. And now the result of this downward course will be seen in that work—which should be the ultimate fruit of the huckleberry field. It will be worthless. It will have none of the spirit of the huckleberry in it, and the reading of it will be a weariness of the flesh. I believe in a different kind of division of labor—that Professor D. should be encouraged to divide himself freely between his library and the huckleberry field. (*Natural History Essays* 250)

Given Thoreau's desire that "there may be as many different persons in the world as possible" (*Walden* 48), the point is not to disparage any particular persons but rather the sort of alienation that results when persons are, again, reduced to functions or to the status of things with a concomitant reduction of their field of perception. The desire for many different persons is in fact a desire for the expansion of perception, consistent with a view that unity exists in multiplicity and diversity, as in his parable of the mountain.

Shifting Roles

As we read Thoreau's natural history writings we find him shifting roles from poet to moralist to naturalist-observer to scientist with some fluidity, often within the same work. What remains consistent is the habit of observation which appears to become both more trained and more diversified over time. The sort of "seeing" that is implied in his assertion that "we must look a long time before we can see" is never identified with any particular vantage but with the training of perception to derive pleasure or knowledge, or pleasure and knowledge combined, from the objects of the beholder's attention. Because Thoreau often drew on prior writing—in his journals and in other works—it is, however, difficult to ascribe changes in approach to his "development" as a writer. It is less difficult to see them as allied to his varied roles in relation to nature: walker, historian, excursionist, surveyor, gardener, and leader of huckleberry parties. These roles allowed him to adopt purposeful or utilitarian approaches to nature, measuring and observing formal relationships in space and time as a surveyor; to ask questions about prior human presence in the landscape, as historian and excursionist; to note the periodicity of natural events by the calendar, as gardener and gatherer; to enjoy the esthetic effects of the natural scene, as walker; and to combine and shift among these modes or approaches almost at will. Overall, they led him to anticipate a sort of interdisciplinary model of inquiry even before the discrete modern disciplines were in fact laid out.

Three passages can perhaps illustrate how modes of representation and thinking in his prose writing about nature make a transit from the highly poetic to the scientific without encountering the sort of dramatic epistemological break or rupture we are accustomed to associate with this span. The first exemplary passage occurs in "Autumnal Tints," which he introduces as a verbal substitute for a preserved leaf collection. (Merely collecting and displaying the diversity of nature was a great aspect of early nineteenth century science, as visitors to older natural history museums know.) Describing a species of red maple common to New England, he writes what we would regard as a poetic tribute:

> The whole tree thus ripening in advance of its fellows attains a singular preeminence, and sometimes maintains it for a week or two. I am thrilled with the sight of it, bearing aloft its scarlet standard for the regiment of green-clad foresters around, and I go a half a mile out my way to examine it. A single tree becomes thus the crowning beauty of some meadowy vale, and the

expression of the whole surrounding forest is at once more spirited for it.

A small red maple has grown perchance, far away at the head of some valley, a mile from any road, unobserved. It has faithfully discharged the duties of a maple there, all winter and summer, neglected none of its economies, but added to its stature in the virtue which belongs to a maple, by a steady growth for so many months, never having gone gadding about, and is nearer heaven than it was in the spring. It has faithfully husbanded its sap, and afforded shelter to a wandering bird, has long since ripened its seeds and committed them to the winds, and has the satisfaction of knowing, perhaps, that a thousand little well-behaved maples are already settled in life somewhere. It deserves well of Mapledom. Its leaves have been asking it from time to time, in a whisper, "When shall we redden?" And now, in this month of September, this month of traveling, when men are hastening to the seaside, or the mountains, or the lakes, this modest maple, still without budging and inch, travels in its reputation,—runs up its scarlet flag on that hillside, which shows that it has finished its summer work before all other trees, and withdraws from the contest. At the eleventh hour of the year, the tree which no scrutiny could have detected here when it was most industrious is thus, by tint of its maturity, by its very blushes, revealed at last to the careless and distant traveler, and leads his thoughts away from the dusty road into those brave solitudes which it inhabits. It flashes out conspicuous with all the virtue and beauty of a maple—Acer rubrum. We may now read its title, or rubric, clear. Its virtues, not its sins, are as scarlet.   (*Natural History Essays* 148-49)

The passage is worth quoting at length to note not so much the presence of an idea (one supposes, perhaps, that trees too are noble after a fashion) as the movement of mind that pursues at some peril a path of invention, fancy, or imagination. Beginning with an observation that could lead to a scientific inquiry—why does just this maple tree turn red before all the others?—Thoreau strikes off on another tangent altogether, deliberately engaging what Matthew Arnold called the "pathetic fallacy" in the manner of a schoolroom composition. But surprisingly the passage coheres. The tree organizes and incites the spectator's perception of the forest around it (a

73

perception rendered abstractly in Wallace Stevens' poem "Anecdote of the Jar") and draws the traveler's thoughts to "brave solitudes." It provides the poet with the opportunity for a run of fancy, turning an object of nature into what is plainly "a kind of fiction, a work of imagination only." That is, as a consciously poetic performance, the passage does not pretend to be anything more or less than an exercise—and I would emphasize the word "exercise"—of the imagination, take it for what you will, but principally for pleasure.

But pleasure, while it sometimes does not lead us to new knowledge, sometimes does. Or at least it may lead us to a surmise that there is knowledge to be had when our attention or our consciousness is arrested by a fact or a "coupling" or assemblage of facts. In a second kind of exemplary passage in "The Natural History of Massachusetts" the basic idea of which Thoreau revised and included in *Walden*, an idea seems to emerge from, rather than to be super-added to, perception:

> When the first rays of the sun slanted over the scene, the grasses seemed hung with innumerable jewels, which jingled merrily as they were brushed by the foot of the traveler, and reflected all the hues of the rainbow, as he moved from side to side. It struck me that these ghost leaves, and the green one whose forms they assume, were the creatures of but one law; that in obedience to the same law the vegetable juices swell gradually into the perfect leaf, on the one hand, and the chrystalline [sic] particles troop to their standard in the same order, on the other. As if the material were indifferent, but the law one and invariable, and every plant in the spring but pushed up into and filled a permanent and eternal mould, which, summer and winter forever, is waiting to be filled.
>
> This foliate structure is common to the coral and the plumage of birds, and to how large a part of animate and inanimate nature. The same independence of law on matter is observable in many other instances, as in the natural rhymes, when some animal form, color, or odor has its counterpart in some vegetable. As, indeed, all rhymes imply an internal melody, independent of any particular sense. (*Natural History Essays* 25)

Here the progress is from the observation of a similarity that could be purely accidental—"innumerable jewels...jingled noisily"—to a surmise—"as if the material were indifferent, but the law one and invariable"—that can be tested by further observation and comparison to see whether it is not the result of any underlying cause or reason. Indeed, the perception of similarity in structure raises the question of the relation of number to sensation, internal to external, object to object, without leading Thoreau hurriedly to specify what the law is outside of his series of comparisons. Critics note that at least in their more elaborate development such passages as this one reflect the influence on Thoreau of Goethe's *Die Italianische Reise* (Walls 34-35), but the formal similarities of crystals and organic forms is still a topic that gives rise to scientific investigation. (In "The Dispersion of Seeds," he would remark "It might be worth the while to inquire why Nature loves the number thirteen in [some just observed] cases" [*Faith in a Seed* 42]. Indeed, such "coincidences" of number and pattern are matters for scientific speculation.)

Observations and couplings of fact such as these gradually accumulated in Thoreau's writing in his notebooks. Observations of weather, the array of plants in the environment, the periodicity of natural events in relation to the calendar, and other natural phenomena absorbed his imagination to the degree that some critics have felt that he must have lost those habits or powers of imagination as he grew older (as though he had grown much older at all, to die at forty-four). Like many writers, perhaps even more than most, Thoreau recycled his writing in and out of texts, published and projected, so that for instance, one meets the passage on leaves and crystals quoted above from "The Natural History of Massachusetts" or another on "the pickerel-fisher" in "A Winter Walk" (*Natural History Essays* 68-69) in a different form in *Walden*. This process was continuing at the end of his life, though it has taken many years for scholars confronting the mass of his writing competently to piece together and perceive how the process was continuing, especially in the period from 1860 to 1862.

The third exemplary passage, in which Thoreau straightforwardly adopts the stance of a naturalist, derives from the reconstruction of a long text that he was working on approximately in 1860-1861. This text, "The Dispersion of Seeds," is thought to have been completed in May 1861, disassembled after his death, and only reconstructed for publication in the 1990s. But it was already pre-figured in the essay which has historically been taken to be Thoreau's chief claim to the status of naturalist, "The Succession of Forest Trees," which he delivered as an address to the Middlesex Agricultural Society in

September 1860 (and published in the *Transactions* of that society). A comparison of the two texts shows how a transition from one state of manuscript, or a composition for one occasion, to that of another, can alter the reader's perception of the intended mode of writing and the depth of thinking that it carries. Here is a passage from the address:

> When, hereabouts, a single forest tree or a forest springs up naturally where none of its kind grew before, I do not hesitate to say, though in some quarters still it may sound paradoxical, that it came from a seed. Of the various ways by which trees are known to be propagated,—by transplanting, cuttings, and the like,—this is the only supposable one under the circumstances. No such tree has ever been known to spring from anything else. If anyone asserts that it sprang from something else, or from nothing, the burden of proof lies with him.
>
> It remains, then, only to show how the seed is transported from where it grows to where it is planted. This is done chiefly by the agency of wind, water, and animals. The light seeds, as those of pines and maples, are transported chiefly by wind and water; the heavier, as acorns and nuts, by animals. (*Natural History Essays* 74)

To some generations of readers who had at least a high school knowledge of botany, this passage, clustered around with quaint and folksy jokes between Thoreau and his audience, must have seemed something of a joke itself—trivial, perverse, unfathomable because not at all deep. (Certainly it seemed so to me. Even after some study I could not understand the game of knowledge that was being played out, or if it was deep or superficial play.) Who would want to demonstrate the obvious? Our own knowledge may obscure for us the meaning of his claim that some may think his theory of seeds "sounds paradoxical." Having learned by rote that "plants come from seeds" or some such, we likely have not thought it was ever a serious question.

In the later reconstruction of the longer text into which Thoreau incorporated this passage a more formal scientific purpose is evident. In "The Dispersion of Seeds," Thoreau begins by noting that the classical writer Pliny "tells us that some trees bear no seed" (*Faith in a Seed* 23), and then states his purpose: "As there is a lingering doubt in many minds with regard to some trees, whether they bear flowers and seed or not, it is the more important to show not only that they do, but for what purpose" (23). There follows an explanation of why, Thoreau supposes, the question has not been attended to, why it is important, and (again) what his purpose is. Only then is the passage that is so peculiar in "Succession" reintroduced in "Dispersion" verbatim. What appears indirect and perhaps even purposeless in the address becomes exemplary of the purpose and method of science. Thoreau then proceeds to comprehensive proof and demonstration, by empirical observation, of the persistence of the principle—the means (by seed), purpose (reproduction), and opportunity (appropriate placement in soil, sun, and water) that support the naturalist's supposition about what is the case. As he proceeds he does not avoid introducing altogether the sort of poetic reflections that color his other writings, but the dominant purpose is still a comprehensive explanation of the dispersion of seeds and the variation or diversity of species in the observed environment. At least one result of his approach, aside from explaining those cases where propagation by seed seems improbable, is to give the sort of picture of the forest environment of his area of New England that he thought was missing from the mere inventory of the government report he had reviewed in "The Natural History of Massachusetts."

The longer and later text methodically develops a relatively technical and practical theory of what biologists would call "speciation" and provides empirical answers to some intuitive but scientifically answerable questions: Why is it that a little red maple will grow alone and thrive at the head of a valley where no other maples are? Why do oaks grow where pine trees were? These answers have applications that are useful. They also simply satisfy our curiosity. They decrease our ignorance of natural, physical processes. But they do not necessarily decrease our wonder or the possibilities for contemplation. Observing the way in which a black willow clings to the bank of the Concord River, "availing itself of every accident to spread along the river's bank," he reflects:

> Heretofore I had ignorantly pitied the hard fate of the tree that was made so brittle and not yielding like a reed. But now I admired its invulnerability [propagating itself by its seeds when twigs break off]. I would gladly hang up my harp on such a willow, if so I might derive inspiration from it. Sitting down by the shore of the Concord, I could almost have wept for joy at the discovery of it. (63)

The ironic allusion to Psalm 137 ("By the waters of Babylon, there we sat down and wept, when we remembered Zion"), a song of captivity, returns us from biological investigation to what is more broadly called "natural history." The allusion reminds us that the trees which have a biological existence in the landscape also have a symbolic and imaginary existence in the discourses of memory. Again, to the naturalist merely, nature can be abstracted as a set of physical processes. But the total of those processes takes place in a context including that of consciousness and historical memory. Strictly speaking, empirical science does not have a theme and its is not itself a philosophy but a method of ascertaining fact. In insisting on incorporating both in his writing, Thoreau abandons neither in the way that the development of the idea of two opposed intellectual cultures—literary and scientific—would seem to imply is necessary.

The core or narrative kernels of Thoreau's writings as a naturalist are stories—for scientists do tell stories about transformations of energy and matter—about the reproduction, differentiation, growth and decay of plants and environments. The essence of the scientist's pursuit—the ability to predict phenomena based on tracing the interrelations of necessary and probable conditions toward particular outcomes through observation and experiment—is incorporated within a concern for the possible forms of existence. This is a matter of theme and of philosophy that is not identical to science itself, since it would be a contradiction to speak of a transcendent science. But the two impulses—toward "knowledge" and toward "sympathy"—are enacted in one frame of discourse in Thoreau's writing. Perhaps it is not too much to say that in bringing together the impulses of different communities of concern, Thoreau is not unlike the ice-fisher who knits together communities where else they would be torn apart. Both the pleasure of reading his work and its possible significance for us derive from this effort—yet another effort to realize the ideal of the one man.

Discussion Questions

1. Consider the comparison in this chapter between scientific reasoning and story-telling. What are the virtues and limitations of this comparison? In what ways are the modes mingled elsewhere in Thoreau's natural history writings? How does the distinction between theme and method lead us to distinguish between story-telling? Does Thoreau's writing benefit from

transgressing the boundary between these two kinds of thinking?
2. Consider Thoreau's use of the word "demoniacal" in the quotation from "The Natural History of Massachusetts" beginning "Slow are the beginnings of philosophy...." Why is such a thinker "demoniacal"? To whom?
3. Is the loss resulting from the division of labor that Thoreau ascribes to the naturalist merely a matter of taste or esthetics or does it have epistemological consequences?

5

Wild Apples,
or the Uses of Thoreau

As He Sowed

It's not books you need, it's some of the things that once were in books. The same things could be in the "parlor families" today. The same infinite detail and awareness could be projected through radios and televisors, but are not. No, no, it's not books at all you're looking for! Take it where you can find it, in old phonograph records, old motion pictures, and in old friends; look for it in nature and look for it in yourself. Books were only one type of receptacle where we stored a lot of things we were afraid we might forget. There is nothing magical in them at all. The magic is only in what books say, how they stitched the patches of the universe together in one garment for us. Of course you couldn't know this, of course you still can't understand what I mean when I say all this. You are intuitively right, that's what counts.   (Faber in Ray Bradbury, *Fahrenheit 451* 82-83)

Each year well more than half a million people turn off a single-digit state highway (Route 2) in Massachusetts onto a three-digit winding road (Route 126) and arrive at Walden Pond, which is now a State Reservation maintained by the Massachusetts Department of

Environmental Management. Having made this trek, you can walk around the perimeter of the pond where you will see others who have come—some with backpacks and books, some with fishing equipment (though fish are reportedly scarce), some (in summer) in swimsuits. You will hear people speak not only English but Italian, German, French, Spanish, Japanese, and other languages of the West and East. Low bushes on sand and gravel banks along the shore are protected by environmentally friendly fencing and embanking beneath mature pines. In late summer you can reach through the fencing and pick low-bush blueberries if someone—bird or person—hasn't beaten you to it. Occasionally, the stillness among the pines and across the pond is broken by the flash and muffled rush of an MBTA commuter train that runs along the roadbed where Thoreau heard the Fitchburg Railway run. Granted that some local people come to the pond simply to swim or fish, and granted that almost any park this close to a major city invites visitors, still others come to pay a sort of indefinite homage. Books and book bags and an uncommon multiplicity of languages are clues that people have something in mind, however indefinite, respecting Thoreau. And an indefinite homage is perhaps the most sincere, one that is most characteristic of a response to the words of what Jaspers calls a paradigmatic individual.

In writing this book, I have tried to avoid citing and discussing a mass of biographical, scholarly, and critical works that would swell its bulk by four or five times. Such a longer book would defeat the publisher's purpose of making a book the reader can easily carry and of keeping its cost low. It might also defeat the purpose of making this a primer on Thoreau, a book that teaches how to read with the goal that the reader will not stop here but go on to read for him or herself, by encumbering it with notations. And so the library is available for further study to us all who are not in prison or some other sort of extremity, and we will see what we can do for those who are. Likewise, although an expectation regarding the ending of this kind of book is that one might trace and evaluate the thinker's influence among many others, I want to mention only a few currents of influence, a few names, to offer a cursory glance at Thoreau's influence. Then, I would like to try to distill something of what I think we can learn from Thoreau, how we can use our reading of him.

Thoreau's influence among social activists is well known. To evaluate what Ghandi, King, and others made of him—how important or incidental Thoreau is to their thinking—would take a larger space than is available here. So is his influence among activists who are

81

concerned with the preservation of nature—from John Muir to later writers such as Loren Eiseley. New influences continue to spring up, such as those among contemporary writers Jane Brox, John Hanson Mitchell, David R. Foster and others as they chronicle subsequent developments in the natural history of Massachusetts. A survey of presumably major influences might lead us to neglect, unless we were being painfully encyclopedic, some odder ones, such as the one that crops up in Ray Bradbury's novel *Fahrenheit 451*, of a half century ago. There Bradbury imagines a counter-culture of Thoreauvian wanderers who memorize books and travel along the edges of cities, not unlike Thoreau's ice-fishers, collectively stitching together the cultural memory that is lost in a society that denies both history and individuality. A much belated transcendentalist, Bradbury imagines a society in which books are banned because they do not agree with each other. "Where's your common sense?" the main character representing this ideology cries, "None of those books agree with each other" (38). In this novel, books represent value and yet, paradoxically, in the passage quoted as the epigraph to this chapter, they are said not to matter at all—not books, not chat rooms (our current equivalent of Bradbury's imagined "parlor family"), not nature, but an indefinite something else, *behind* them.

Thoreau was as well read in world literature, often in its original languages, as nearly anyone in his own time. His concern with books was much like his concern with fruits, not that they should conform to one type, but that they should proliferate truths and be various; not that they should lead one to think the one true thing, but that they should lead one to think at all and have some bloom and progeny. One can take from his own writing sayings that will support contrasting points of view—as, for example, one can discern right-wing and left-wing interpreters of his writing—and not get a view of the whole. He scorned a mere reliance on the inherited verbal forms of the past, but few writers read as deeply as he did in the histories of his region—covering the two hundred years before his own awareness of the grass growing in the fields of Concord—and of the changes in the land that resulted from the human presence in it. He was not a religionist, but few writers have worked (as I hope to have suggested) so assiduously to transform the reported words of Jesus and the Judeo-Christian scriptures into a form of thought that was useful to his day.

These are apparent paradoxes. So one finds many commentators on Thoreau perplexed, and many imagine him either a blithe free spirit or a cantankerous critic, without being able to imagine beyond the appearance of a polarity or contradiction or even to attend to disparate facts. Faced with apparent paradox, the middle way is not always the best. Rhetorically handy as it is, especially when one tries to bring writers into some sort of mainstream of culture or to make them conform to our institutional expectations, the approach sometimes fails. Thus, it is misleading to say, as one commentator does in a popular reference work, "Thoreau's stance was always much less extreme than many of his individual, sometimes inconsistent statements suggest" (Wagenknecht 1076). This statement is made about a writer who said "my thoughts are murder to the State" at a moment when he knew that such a statement could be construed not merely as extreme or unfriendly to the powers that be but as treason and a capital offense.

It is necessary to be uncompromising here. It is not the way of the middle of the road to harbor a "fugitive slave" or to go to prison, even for a day, for purposefully and on the basis of principle refusing to pay one's taxes, even if we think it is the right thing to do. It is not moderation to say, "Break the law." Thoreau was a radical thinker and actor, and one must take him as such or not at all. With some it is necessary to make the same point about Thoreau that Thoreau made about John Brown: It is possible to be intransigently radical and yet quite sane.

He was also passionately concerned to understand the significance of the "human entity" in nature, in some of the larger ways that I have attempted to outline in previous chapters, and more locally. In works that are not treated here, he extended his concern with the moral quality of the human presence in North America, and not only that of Europeans but also that of Native Americans and African Americans. The span of time between the beginning of the first continuous European settlements in his locality (1620-1640) and his own (1817-1862) was in fact somewhat longer than the span of time between his time and our own. Yet we are likely to imagine him—and traditions of scholarly criticism have confirmed this imagining—as among the first "permanent" or classic American writers. Surveying in Concord or Haverhill, Massachusetts, or Perth Amboy, New Jersey, he observed the remnants of those settlements and behind and beneath them those of prior inhabitants already routed from the premises. On his travels to Maine, he observed the remnants of New England tribes. At the end of his life, out of concern for his health and a long held interest in Native Americans he traveled to Minnesota with Horace Mann and met with displaced "Indians." As he tried to understand something of the relations among European languages, he tried to understand something of the Algonquian. In his own imagination, he was at the beginning of a possible history (as the ending of several of his works suggest) and at the end of others which others had lived. Yet, for reasons outlined briefly in Chapter 4, his possible contribution to the reflective natural history of the human presence in North America was deflected and he was relegated to the status of being a passionate poet of wildness and wilderness only.

Thoreau's pre-eminent modern biographer, Robert D. Richardson, Jr., writes in his introduction to *Faith in a Seed*, that there emerges from Thoreau's last work "a powerful metaphor of death and rebirth" ("Thoreau's Broken Task" 16). In some small part, we have seen this metaphoric transition enacted in the works we have read. But comforting as the idea of a cycle of death and rebirth is, it loses some of its force for "human entities" if it does not admit the possibility of some residual that does not get recycled. That is, no thinker can be great who does not encounter strenuously the idea that some change and loss is permanent and absolute. Where nothing can be lost and nothing gained, change is meaningless and, in effect, only a transposition of finite elements in a finite scheme. It is for that reason, I think, that such metaphors emerge either "tentatively and incompletely," as Richardson describes them in the late work of "The Dispersion of Seeds," or as the flash of a sort of future hope in others. Metaphors of rebirth struggle with a latent awareness of the permanence of loss and change as poignant as any in American literature.

This is true in another late manuscript which was published shortly after Thoreau's death (in *The Atlantic Monthly*, November 1862), where Thoreau describes a predicament of things passing that will not return, things that involve both entities and relationships. The essay is called "Wild Apples," and it indicates how Thoreau was aware of living in human history and in an environment in which the thought and will of human beings had an effect on the conditions of their lives—whatever wilderness or wildness might surround their communities. His words conclude with this elegiac paragraph:

> The era of the Wild Apple will soon be past. It is a fruit which will probably become extinct in New England. You may still wander through old orchards of native fruit of great extent, which for the most part went to the cider-mill, now all gone to decay. I have heard of an orchard in a distant town, on the side of a hill,

where the apples rolled down and lay four feet deep against a wall on the lower side, and this the owner cut down for fear they would be made into cider. Since the temperance reform and the general introduction of grafted fruit, no native apple trees, such as I see everywhere in deserted pastures, and where the woods have grown up around them, are set out. I fear that he who walks over these fields a century hence will not know the pleasure of knocking off wild apples. Ah, poor man, there are many pleasures which he will not know! Notwithstanding the prevalence of the Baldwin and the Porter [varieties of apples], I doubt if so extensive orchards are set out today as there were a century ago, when those vast straggling cider-orchards were planted, when men both ate and drank apples, when the pomace-heap was the only nursery, and trees cost nothing but the trouble of setting them out. Men could afford then to stick a tree by every wall-side and let it take its chance. I see nobody planting trees to-day in such out of the way places, along the lonely roads and lanes, and at the bottom of dells in the wood. Now that they have grafted trees, and pay a price for them, they collect them into a plat by their houses, and fence them,—and the end of it all will be that we shall be compelled to look for our apples in a barrel. (*Natural History Essays* 209).

The prophecy has come to pass, of course, while Thoreau's elegiac words (principally from his first book, *A Week on the Concord and Merrimack Rivers*) are resurrected in a contemporary book on the passing of family farms and orchards into oblivion, Jane Brox's *Five Thousand Days Like This One*. Brox tells the story of the development and decline of a Lebanese family's farm in Middlesex County, adding another chapter to the history of nature and human habitation in the landscape Thoreau had begun. But what are apples or Broxes to us if the metaphorical barrel at the supermarket provides? "Poor man, there are many pleasures which he will not know!" Not knowing what those pleasures might have been, one perhaps feels no loss, but the passage does ask us to meditate on loss—whether it be a merely speculative loss (the loss of some pleasure one has never known, and so does not feel) or the loss, if you will permit, of a sense of loss. If we think that Thoreau was egotistical, as some have clearly done, why do we think he worries over the possible loss to be experienced by others whom he could never know? Put another way, why write of pleasure unless one's own pleasure is enhanced by that of others? Why write of a change in the conditions of life unless to exemplify and warn that such change may come?

Thoreau's text in "Wild Apples" does not end with his own words, but with a long quotation from the Book of Joel (1.2, 1.4-7, 1.11a) in which the speaker laments:

> The vine is dried up, and the fig tree languisheth; the pomegranate tree, the palm tree also, and the apple tree, even all the trees of the field, are withered because joy is withered away from the sons of men. (Joel 1.12)

The aptness of the fruit symbolism is apparent, but it is perhaps remarkable that Thoreau does not turn the trope of withering toward one of rebirth, as Joel himself does. The Book of Joel is a minor prophecy, and may seem like an odd byway, apart from apples, for Thoreau to choose. But it was a common text to be cited in Puritan sermons of polity, such as Winthrop's "A Model of Christian Charity" (alluding to "make not thy heritage a reproach, a byword among nations" 2.17), and it was ironically apt at the onset of the Civil War ("Beat your plowshares into swords" 3.10a). Moreover, it opens with the command to tell the history of these people: "Hath this been in your days, or even in the days of your fathers? Tell your children of it, and let their children tell their children and their children another generation"(1.2b-3). Take it for what one will, the Hebrew and Puritan prophets alike, whatever their understanding of the fate of individuals, understand that the fate of communities are complex matters of will, historical opportunity, intelligence, and something else that transcends the finite elements ("facts") known from the past. And Thoreau affirms the idea of community by telling stories.

Thoreau liked "to link" his "facts to fable" in order I think (to borrow again from Wordsworth) to connect the "individual and local" with the "general and operative" ("Preface" *Lyrical Ballads* 257). Another name for the linking of fact and fable is history. And though he seems often to have wanted to put his history into the shape and form of a fable of redemption—resurrection and rebirth, he also related those histories that end rather in deliquescence (those, for instance, of the "Former Inhabitants" of the vicinity of Walden) or in tragedy. Indeed, against the powerful impulse toward creating a redemptive myth, he writes in *Walden* that "when the play, it may be the tragedy, of life is over, the spectator goes his way" (91). There is a complex myth or fable that vies with death and rebirth throughout his work—that works its way through the text of "The Dispersion of Seeds." It is that life is a matter of pattern and predictability coupled with contingency. Natural science, indeed, could tell us that—and we might say, like Thoreau, that it is only a restatement of fact. In linking such fact to fable the aspect of contingency—"the play [play as literary artifact or children's game?], it may be the tragedy [another work of imagination only or something more real]"—is the hinge that connects history and transcendence. Oddly, it also links his thinking back to one of the primary and enduring fables of those works which he alludes to most frequently, the parables of Jesus in the gospels:

> And as he sowed some seed fell by the wayside; and the birds came and devoured them. Some fell on stony places, where they did not have much earth; and they immediately sprang up because they had no depth of earth. But when the sun was up they were scorched, and because they had no root they were withered away. And some fell among thorns, and the thorns sprang up and choked them. But others fell on good ground and yielded a crop: some a hundredfold, some sixty, some thirty. He who has ears to hear, let him hear! (Matthew 13.4-9; cf. Mark 4.2-20 and Luke 8.5-8)

This passage (one of only seven parables to appear in each of the three parabolic gospels) is followed by Jesus' explanation to his disciples of why he chooses not to speak more plainly. Despite the plainness of its metaphors, it remains opaque and troubling. For the naturalist's explanation of the overabundance of seed among trees and other plants seems to make sense. But what is the mystery of the over-abundance of human entities in relation to the resources of happiness or intelligence or freedom or other values? It may strike us a little compellingly that this parable figures the biblical precept ultimately interpreted by Cowper in his own figures in "The Cast-Away," where the stony heart of the castaway cannot soften to receive the seed and neither does the sea buoy it up.

Surely these words lead us to consider the complex elements of our own fates—whether similar to that imagined by a Cowper, Melville, or Thoreau, or something altogether different. So too Thoreau asks us to consider what the conditions of our lives, individually and collectively are—what the conditions of any life are—and what sort of life we would choose when we have the opportunity to choose one consistent with "simplicity, independence, magnanimity, and trust" (*Walden* 9). He does not, indeed, found a school or prescribe a form of thought but teaches in the best and most generous sense by leading us out and inciting us to think, to engage in dialogue: For how many questions does he ask, after all, of his readers—as though he were not just being rhetorical but searching for response?

Discussion Questions

1. List the questions that Thoreau asks in any chapter of *Walden* or in any of his essays. Does his mode of questioning support the idea that he is an effective teacher? Based on your observations about his use of questions, parables, or other rhetorical or stylistic features, how would you compare his persona as a teacher with that of any of Jaspers' paradigmatic individuals: Socrates, Buddha, Confucius, Jesus?
2. Consult the work of any of the authors mentioned in this chapter as being influenced by Thoreau (see "Works Cited" for further references) and discuss how they reflect his influence. Discuss his influence on these or any other writers with whom you are familiar.
3. In nearly all of his writings—certainly in all modes of his writing—Thoreau employs allusions to the Bible and particularly to the New Testament. Are there characteristic types of passages he alludes to in distinct modes—natural history writing, social reform writing, and reflective philosophical writing? Does there appear to be a method to his choice of passages to allude to?

Works Cited

Beadle, John. *Journal or Diary of a Thankful Christian* [1656]. Quoted in Sacvan Bercovitch. *Puritan Origins of the American Self.* New Haven: Yale UP, 1975: 40.

Bickman, Martin. Walden: *Volatile Truths.* New York: Twayne, 1992.

Bradbury, Ray. *Fahrenheit 451* [1950]. New York: Ballantine, 1996.

Briggs, Charles Frederick. "A Yankee Diogenes." *Putnam's Monthly Magazine* 4 (1854) 443-48. Rpt. In Thoreau, *Walden*: 314-17.

Brox, Jane. *Five Thousand Days Like This One: An American Family History.* Boston: Beacon, 1999.

Bunyan, John. *The Pilgrim's Progress* [1678]. Ed. Catharine Stimpson. New York: New American Library, 1964.

Cavell, Stanley. "Captivity and Despair in *Walden* and "Civil Disobedience." In Thoreau, *Walden*, Ed. William Rossi: 390-405.

---------. *The Senses of* Walden. New York: Viking, 1972.

Cowper, William. *The Cast-away: The Text of the Original Manuscript.* Ed. Charles Ryskamp. Princeton: Princeton Univ. Library, 1963.

Derrida, Jacques. "Before the Law." In *Acts of Literature*. Ed. Derek Attridge. New York: Routledge, 1992: 181-220.

Donahue, Brian. *Reclaiming the Commons: Community Farms and Forests in a New England Town.* New Haven: Yale UP, 1999.

Douglass, Frederick. *Narrative of the Life of Frederick Douglass, an American Slave* [1845]. Ed. Houston A. Baker, Jr. New York: Penguin, 1982.

Emerson, Ralph Waldo. *Essays and Lectures.* Ed. Joel Porte. New York: Library of America, 1983.

---------. "Thoreau" [1862]. In Thoreau. *Walden.* Ed. William Rossi: 320-333.

"Enoch." *Harper's Bible Dictionary.* Ed. Miller and Miller. New York: Harper, 1961.

Foster. David R. *Thoreau's Country: Journey through a Transformed Landscape.* Cambridge: Harvard UP, 1999.

Jaspers, Karl. *Socrates, Buddha, Confucius, Jesus: The Paradigmatic Individuals.* [*The Great Philosophers* Vol. 1]. Ed. Hannah Arendt. Trans. Ralph Manheim. New York: Harcourt Brace, 1962.

Hegel, G.W.F. *The Phenomenology of Mind* [1807]. Trans. J. B. Baillie. New York: Harper and Row, 1967.

Hobbes, Thomas. *Leviathan* [1651]. Ed. J.C.A. Gaskin. Oxford: Oxford UP, 1996.

Hume, David. *A Treatise of Human Nature* [1739]. Ed. L.A. Selby Bigge. Oxford: Oxford UP, 1973.

Marx, Karl. *Capital* [1867]. Trans. Samuel Moore and Edward Aveling [1887]. In Robert C. Tucker, ed. *The Marx-Engels Reader.* New York: W.W. Norton, 1972: 191-318.

Melville, Herman. *Moby-Dick; or, The Whale* [1851]. Northwestern-Newberry Edition. Ed. Harrison Hayford et al. Chicago: Northwestern UP and Newberry Library, 1988.

--------. "The Portent." *Poems of Herman Melville.* Ed. Douglas Robillard. Albany: New College and UP, 1976: 34.

Milton, John. "Areopagitica" [1644]. In *John Milton: Selected Prose.* Ed. C.A. Patrides. Hammondsworth: Penguin, 1974: 196-248.

Mitchell, John Hanson. *Walking Towards Walden: A Pilgrimage in Search of Place.* Reading, MA: Addison-Wesley, 1995.

Mulloney, Stephen. *Traces of Thoreau: A Cape Cod Journey.* Boston: Northeastern UP, 1998.

Poirier, Richard. *A World Elsewhere: The Place of Style in American Literature.* New York: Oxford UP, 1966.

Radhakrishnan, Sarvepalli, and Charles R. Moore, eds. *A Sourcebook in Indian Philosophy.* Princeton: Princeton UP, 1957.

Richardson, Robert D., Jr. *Henry Thoreau: A Life of the Mind.* Berkeley: Univ. of California P, 1986.

--------. "Thoreau's Broken Task." In Thoreau, *Faith in a Seed*: 3-17.

Shakespeare, William. *Coriolanus* [1608]. In *Complete Works of William Shakespeare.* Ed. Craig and Bevington. Glenview, IL: Scott, Foresman, 1973: 1108-1147.

Stevens, Wallace. "Anecdote of the Jar." *Complete Poems.* New York: Knopf, 1976.

Thoreau, Henry David. *Faith in a Seed: "The Dispersion of Seeds" and Other Late Natural History Writings.* Ed. Bradley P. Dean. Washington, DC: Island, 1993.

--------. *The Natural History Essays.* Ed. Robert Sattlemeyer. Salt Lake: Peregrine Smith, 1980.

--------. *Reform Papers.* Ed. Wendell Glick. Princeton: Princeton UP, 1973.

--------. *Transmigration of the Seven Brahmans* [c. 1849-59]. Ed. Arthur Christy. New York: Haskell, 1972.

--------. Walden *and "Resistance to Civil Government."* Norton Critical Edition. Second Edition. Ed. William Rossi. New York: W.W. Norton, 1966.

--------. *A Week on the Concord and Merrimack Rivers* [1849]. In *Henry David Thoreau: A Week...*, Ed. Robert F. Sayre. New York: Library of America, 1985: 1-319.

Von Frank, Albert J. *The Trials of Anthony Burns: Freedom and Slavery in Emerson's Boston.* Cambridge: Harvard UP, 1998.

Wagenknecht, Edward. "Thoreau, Henry David." In *The Reader's Companion to American History.* Ed. Eric Foner and John A. Garraty. Boston: Houghton Mifflin, 1991: 1076.

Walls, Laura Dassow. *Seeing New Worlds: Henry David Thoreau and Nineteenth-Century Natural Science.* Madison: Univ. of Wisconsin P, 1995.

White, E. B. "*Walden*—1954." In Thoreau, *Walden.* Ed. Rossi: 359-366.

Williams, William Carlos. *The Collected Poems of William Carlos Williams: Volume I, 1909-1939.* Ed. A. Walton Litz and Christopher McGowan. New York: New Directions, 1986.

Wilson, Edward O. *Consilience: The Unity of Knowledge.* New York: Random House, 1998.

Wittgenstein, Ludwig. *Wittgentstein's* Tractatus. Trans. Daniel Kolak. Mountain View, CA: Mayfield, 1998.

Wordsworth, William. "Preface." *Lyrical Ballads* [1802]. In Wordsworth and Coleridge, *Lyrical Ballads.* Second Edition. Ed. R.L. Brett and A.R. Jones. London: Routledge, 1991.

--------. "Preface." *Poems* [1815]. Vol. I. London: Longman, 1815: vii-xlii.

--------. "The World is Too Much with Us." *Poems* [1815]. Vol. II. London: Longman: 182.